Light Through the Spectrum

Essays on Biblical Counseling

Michael R. Burgos

Chris Chumita

Published by

CHURCH MILITANT
PUBLICATIONS
Artillery Support for the Local Church

Torrington, Connecticut, USA

ISBN: 9798681838241

CONTENTS

Essays on Biblical Counseling

ix

A Note to the Reader

Now in its third generation, the biblical counseling movement has increased in diversity, breadth, and affirmation among conservative Protestants. We have a great appreciation for this movement and cast our lot in with those who, having been convicted of the sufficiency of the Word of God, have sought to counsel from the Scriptures. With great appreciation, we have striven to understand the biblical counseling movement, its interlocutors and its implications. This volume is comprised of the best of our reflections and we pray that you will find these edifying and worth your consideration.

Over the course of years, I have grown increasingly interested in the intersection of biblical counseling, theological polemics, and systematic theology. My contributions to this volume primarily focus on these areas and reveal my affinity for the first generation of biblical counselors. By contrast, Chumita's contributions are constructive, succinct, and, in my estimation, very helpful. He has provided a concise summary of the movement and an insightful consideration of counseling from the abundant resources of the Old Testament.

As this book approached publishing we received news that Dr. Jay E. Adams has gone on to be with our Lord. Whereas my coauthor and I have never had the privilege of personally knowing Dr. Adams, we feel as though we do; for this work wouldn't exist without his faithfulness to Christ's church. I recall many days pouring over his books and praising God for the encouragement and conviction therein. His text *More Than Redemption* still remains a formative one for me and one that has indelibly marked the minds of many. We give thanks for the life and ministry of Dr. Adams and we trust that his bold and relentless stand for the gospel and the sufficiency of Scripture will endure, inspiring generations to come.

M. R. Burgos
Torrington, CT
December 2020

1

A Brief Overview of the Biblical Counseling Movement

Chris Chumita

Introduction

In 1970, the church experienced a modern reformation in the area of biblical counseling. In a way, the publication of Jay Adams' landmark book, *Competent to Counsel*, was not unlike Martin Luther's nailing of the Ninety-Five Theses to the door of the Castle Church in Wittenberg.[1] Just like Luther, Adams unapologetically called the

---

[1] The concept of comparing Jay Adams to Martin Luther is not new. It has been discussed in different articles, lectures, and conversations (e.g., Jim Newheiser, 10/30/2017, "Martin Luther and Jay Adams," *Association of Certified Biblical Counselors*, https://biblicalcounseling.com/adams-and-juther/.

church back to the Bible. He took the battle cry of the Reformation, *sola Scriptura*, and applied it to counseling. His insistence on the sufficiency of Scripture, and his unique personality, were the catalysts that triggered the biblical counseling movement (BCM). While the BCM began with the publication of *Competent to Counsel*, the concept was not new. God has always empowered his shepherds to care for the needs and souls of his sheep with his Word. Unfortunately, there have been periods where his people swayed from using the Scriptures in counseling, but God has faithfully always called his people back to the Word.

To understand the BCM, we must first define biblical counseling and briefly examine how the Bible was used to counsel God's people in the past. Thereafter we will explore God's sovereign hand in using sinful men to call the church back to the sufficiency of Scripture and examine the BCM's theological advancements as well as various threats to the movement. Due to the BCM's extensive history and deeply theological nature, this chapter can only briefly examine some of the highlights of its history and will provide only a cursory examination of some of its theological distinctives.

WHAT IS BIBLICAL COUNSELING?

True biblical counseling is a methodology that openly affirms the sufficiency of the Scripture for the counseling task. It holds that the Scriptures are the ultimate authority in counseling and that authentic change can only be affected by the work of the Holy Spirit. This view of counseling is based upon a variety of biblical passages, including 2 Timothy 3:16-17 and 1 Peter 1:20-21. Until recently, it was referred to as Nouthetic Counseling. The word "Nouthetic" is based on the Greek words *nouthesis* and *noutheteo*. According to Adams:

> The word comes from the Greek New Testament. It has, within it, three elements-*concern, confrontation,* and *change*. Nouthetic counseling is counseling that involves face to face confrontation by one person to another, out of loving concern for him, in order to bring about the changes God desires in his life.[2]

Biblical counseling is unashamedly Christ-centered. Adams rightly wrote, "Jesus Christ is at the center of all true Christian counseling. Any counseling which moves Christ from that position of centrality has to the extent that it has done so ceased to be Christian."[3] Therefore, biblical counselors strongly reject integrating secular psychology into their counseling methodology. While biblical counselors may utilize other Christian resources such as books, confessions, catechisms, videos, and songs while counseling someone, those resources will always be subservient to Scripture.

One of the main distinctives of biblical counseling is its recognition that every problem experienced by humanity is due to sin in some way. One's

---

[2] Jay Adams, *What is Nouthetic Counseling?* http://www.nouthetic.org/what-is-nouthetic-counseling.

[3] Jay Adams, *Competent to Counsel*, (Grand Rapids, MI: Zondervan, 1970), 41.

problem may be due to his sin, someone else's sin, or it may be derivative of the fall. However, even if he is a victim, he is still responsible to respond to his circumstance in a God-honoring fashion. The fact that a person's problem is ultimately owed to sin actually provides an avenue for true hope since there is a cure in Jesus Christ.

Another major distinctive of biblical counseling is that it is meant to be church-based, where both the counselor and counselee are under the authority of a local church. As a result, the counselor is a pastor, or someone called by the church leadership, to serve in that capacity. In this environment, loving church discipline can be a powerful tool in the counseling process.

Biblical counseling is a ministry of the Word of God and is one of the ordinary means of grace. J. Ryan Davidson rightly notes that "The ministry of the word is not just for unbelieving sinners who need to trust in Jesus. The ministry of the word is of continued necessity for the believer as well."[4] Since biblical counseling is one of the ordinary means of grace, it cannot be neglected. Mark Mann has noted:

> The ministry of God's Word takes place primarily in the church in a variety of different ways: from the pulpit, in the classroom, in the counseling office and in Christian homes. With the divine mandate to save men from their lost

---

[4] J. Ryan Davidson, *Green Pastures: A Primer on the Ordinary Means of Grace* (Palmdale, CA: Reformed Baptist Academic Press, 2019), 35.

state and transform them into the likeness of Christ, the church has been entrusted with this great responsibility by God's power to His glory.[5]

IS BIBLICAL COUNSELING NEW?

The concept of using the Bible as the only inerrant and sufficient source to minister to God's people was not invented by Adams. The church has an illustrious history of wielding the Scriptures to personally minister to hurting people; albeit, the formality of biblical counseling has changed over time.

MARTIN LUTHER AND COUNSELING

When one thinks of biblical counseling throughout the history of the church, Martin Luther is not the first name that comes to mind; however, Luther made major contributions to pastoral biblical counseling. Pastor and author Bob Kelleman stated,

The person who has most impacted my understanding and practice of counseling is Martin Luther."[6] According to Kelleman, "While we see Luther as a theologian-reformer, he envisioned himself as a pastor-counselor. In this calling, Luther engaged both in pulpit ministry of the Word—preaching, and in [the] personal

---

[5] Mark Mann, *One Ministry of the Word* (Stanley, NC: Timeless Texts, 2004), vii-viii.

[6] Bob Kellemen, *Counseling Under the Cross: How Martin Luther Applied the Cross to Daily Life* (Greensboro, NC: New Growth Press, 2017), 3.

ministry of the Word—counseling.[7]

Luther was a master at taking what Jesus Christ accomplished on the cross and using it to minister to the struggling Christian. People who have studied his works and his counseling methodology describe it as grace-filled and note that it consistently points the Christian to Christ instead of to themselves. Unfortunately, Luther is more known for his harsh rebukes than his tender shepherding.

THE PURITANS

The Puritans were Protestant ministers in the 16th and 17th centuries who sought to purify the church of ungodly practices and influences. They were "masters at understanding the nature of human beings and applying Scripture in practical ways to help people with their struggles and problems."[8] The Puritans are often referred to as "Physicians of the Soul" because "they were sound theologically but did not stop with just propounding theological truth or doctrine, rather they made those doctrines functional in the day to day struggles of the people they taught."[9]

The Puritans were prolific—writing books and tracts that provided instruction and comfort for Christians who were struggling with various sins and trials. For example, *Lifting Up for the Downcast* by William Bridge

---

[7] Ibid., 44-5.

[8] Mark Deckard, *Helpful Truth in Pat Places: The Puritan Practice of Biblical Counseling* (Ross-shire, Great Britain: Christian Focus Publications, 2010), 9.

[9] Ibid., 11.

dealt with the common issue of depression, Jeremiah Burroughs addressed discontentment in The *Rare Jewel of Christian Contentment*, and Thomas Brooks discussed assurance of salvation in *Heaven on Earth*. The most well-known counseling book from the Puritan era is *The Christian Directory* by Richard Baxter. It addressed numerous problems that Christians face in their daily lives and it is often described as an early counseling manual. Baxter was well-known for practicing what he wrote and taught about the private ministry of the Word. He had a reputation for faithfully visiting the homes of the people under his care and helping them apply to the Word of God to their problems.

ICHABOD SPENCER

Ichabod Spencer (1798 – 1854) was a congregational pastor in Northampton, Massachusetts, in the very church that was once pastored by Jonathan Edwards. He later served a congregation in New York where he was affectionately referred to as the "Bunyan of Brooklyn" due to his devotion to the Lord and his deep concern for the lost.

Over the course of his ministerial service, Spencer visited the homes of every one of his church members on a yearly basis and had countless conversations with lost and weary souls. He recorded many of the conversations in what he referred to as "Sketches." Spencer published *A Pastor's Sketches* at the urging of his friends and it is considered to be the last widely published work in the field of biblical counseling for a significant period of time. Spencer hoped that his work:

> ...might be instructive by showing the application of divine truth to human hearts – by leading some anxious inquirers after salvation to see what it is that hinders them from peace with God – and by leading private Christians and young ministers of the gospel to study more carefully what they say to those, who inquire what they shall do to be saved.[10]

THE DARK YEARS

After the publication of Spencer's *A Pastor's Sketches*, the personal ministry of the Word of God fell into an extended period of theological neglect. While there are multiple reasons to explain why the church lost its focus on the personal ministry of the Word, space will only allow us to briefly address three of them.

The first reason for the neglect of the personal ministry of the Word was the revivalism of the 1700s. Lambert rightly pointed out that revivalism and counseling have opposite emphases.[11] Revivalism focused on attracting large crowds, public preaching, and in some cases, superficial decisions for Christ. Counseling, on the other hand, is focused on ministering to individuals and is committed to what can often be a

---

[10] Ichabod Spencer, *A Pastor's Sketches: Conversations with Anxious Souls Concerning the way of Salvation* (Vestavia Hills, AL: Solid Ground Christian Books, 2013), 1.

[11] Heath Lambert, *The Biblical Counseling Movement After Adams* (Wheaton, IL: Crossway, 2012), 29.

long process of helping a Christian conquer sin.

The second reason for the neglect of the personal ministry of the Word was the Fundamentalist-Modernist Controversy that occurred at the end of the nineteenth century. The church's attention and focus were consumed with defending the core truths of the Christian faith against liberalism. "This left an opening for the modernists to come in and take over counseling within the church."[12]

The third reason for the neglect of the personal ministry of the Word was the psychological revolution that attacked "while the church was grappling with revivalism and modernism."[13] Since its inception psychologists, like Sigmund Freud, set out to remove counseling from a ministerial context and place it into a secular one.[14] The psychologists were successful beyond what anyone could have imagined. Their theories were quickly accepted by society as a science and many pastors quickly handed over their responsibility to secular therapists.

JAY ADAMS: THE FOUNDER OF THE MODERN BIBLICAL COUNSELING MOVEMENT

Adams was born on January 30th, 1929 to a non-religious family in Maryland. After his conversion, Adams felt an immediate call to ministry and enrolled at the Reformed Episcopal Seminary in Philadelphia. He

---

[12] Lambert, *The Biblical Counseling Movement After Adams*, 31.

[13] Ibid., 31.

[14] Ibid., 32.

served in various ministerial roles until he was ordained by the United Presbyterian Church in 1952.

Adams served as a pastor for several different congregations over the next few years. His time in the pastorate was tumultuous due to numerous church conflicts, church splits, and denominational strife. He furthered his education by studying at John Hopkins University, Temple University School of Theology, and the University of Missouri before he accepted a position as a special lecturer in Practical Theology at Westminster Theological Seminary in 1963. While at Westminster Adams "was assigned to teach courses on public speaking, preaching, and poimenics. The poimenics course contained a unit on counseling."[15]

The Birth of the Modern Biblical Counseling Movement

While a professor at Westminster Theological Seminary, Adams was unable to find material for the counseling unit that was solidly Christian. Over the next few years, Adams struggled to develop a Christian approach to counseling that was faithful to the Word of God as well as to his Reformed theology; however, he grappled with the degree to which pastors should counsel. Oddly enough, God used a secular psychologist named O. Hobart Mowrer to open his eyes and help him develop a truly biblical model of counseling.

Adams attended a lecture by the anti-Freudian psychologist Mowrer at the urging of a friend, and he was

---

[15] David Powlison, *The Biblical Counseling Movement* (Greensboro, NC: New Growth Press, 2010), 34.

mesmerized by Mowrer's radically different views. Even though he was not a Christian, Mowrer believed that people were morally responsible for their actions and would refer to certain behaviors as sin. He also openly attacked the widely popular Freudian theory.

At Mowrer's suggestion, Adams participated in several week-long internships with Mowrer at different state mental hospitals. During the internship, Adams witnessed Mowrer authoritatively confront the sinful behavior of the patients and call them to change their behavior. Mowrer even encouraged patients to find a way to pay restitution to the people they had hurt. Mowrer's approach was effective, but Adams recognized that his patients were only experiencing a superficial change. His experience with Mowrer was just what Adams needed to dig into the Bible and develop the methodology that would become the BCM.

In 1966, Adams was given a full-time assistant professorship at Westminster and was charged with teaching pastoral theology. Within two years his unit on counseling became an entire course. During this period, Adams partnered with a pastor named Gardner McBride to start the Christian Counseling and Education Center (CCEC). CCEC was a counseling center that was based in Gardner's church that focused on training pastors to counsel. Two years later CCEC was rebranded as the Christian Counseling and Education Foundation (CCEF). CCEF expanded the ministry beyond what it was as CCEC by expanding the ministry beyond Gardner's church. John Bettler, a Presbyterian pastor, was chosen to lead CCEF.

It was during this era that Adams turned his

counseling curriculum into a book which he called *Competent to Counsel*. This volume is credited as the official beginning of the BCM and was a runaway bestseller among evangelicals. *Competent to Counsel* sold over 250,000 copies in the 1970s alone.[16] David Powlison remarked that "The publication of *Competent to Counsel* in 1970 marked the inception of a discernable nouthetic counseling movement and triggered lively controversy in the evangelical community."[17]

People who read *Competent to Counsel* seemed to react in one of two ways. Christian psychologists and integrationists saw it as a dangerous movement that caused Christians to turn to untrained pastors instead of to trained professionals for help for serious problems. Other people read it and ran back to the truths of Scripture as the authoritative source to help Christians with their problems. It also inspired pastors to return to the private ministry of the Word.

In the early 1970s, Bill Goode, a Baptist pastor from Indiana, and Bob Smith, a physician, came under the influence of Adams. Both men had become disillusioned by the Christian psychology movement. Over the next few years, Goode and Smith established Faith Baptist Counseling Ministry (FBCM) with the help of Bettler. FBCM was under the oversight of Goode's church, Faith Baptist Church located in Lafayette, Indiana. "Smith,

---

[16] Powlison, *The Biblical Counseling Movement*, 6.

[17] Ibid., 51. See also Edward Welch and David Powlison, 1997, "Every Common Bush Afire With God: The Scripture's Constitutive Role for Counseling," *Journal of Psychology and Christianity,* 16:4, 304.

Goode, and the FBVM staff would go on to train more than one thousand pastors and missionaries between 1973 and the early 1990s, as well as conducting scores of seminars throughout the United States."[18]

In 1973, John Broger was serving as the highest-ranking civilian employee in the United States Armed Forces when he was introduced to Adams' work.[19] He quickly became a convert and used his influence to hold a seminar by Adams for military chaplains. Broger then used the materials from the seminar to create a *Self-Confrontation Manual* and training courses. Over the next fifteen years, more than 100,000 copies of the manual were distributed to students who took training courses.[20] Broger expanded his views beyond those of Adams, but stuck to the core truths of biblical counseling.[21] While Adams' focus was on training pastors, Broger focused on training the average Christian in the pew. He can rightly be credited with helping spread Adams' message beyond the pastor's office.

In 1976, Bettler's dream of creating an accrediting body for the BCM was finally realized. The National Association of Nouthetic Counselors (NANC) was formed under the protective arm of CCEF. NANC had numerous responsibilities including setting standards for the fledgling movement, accrediting training centers, and certifying individuals.

---

[18] Powlison, *The Biblical Counseling Movement*, 58.

[19] Ibid., 61.

[20] Ibid., 63.

[21] The differences between Adams and Broger could not be explored in further detail due to the scope of the chapter and space constraints.

After two years of existence, NANC started the process of breaking away from CCEF and slowly became its own entity. Initially, the idea of certification did not seem to take off despite the widespread interest in biblical counseling. NANC did not even reach one hundred members until sometime in the early 1980s.[22] In 2013, NANC would change its name to the Association of Certified Biblical Counselors (ACBC).

STAGNATION OF THE BIBLICAL COUNSELING MOVEMENT

Despite the blessing of seeing rapid and explosive growth in the early years, the BCM soon hit what appeared to be a dead end. According to Cameron Fraser, "The movement stagnated in the eighties as the evangelical psychotherapeutic 'counterinsurgency' responded and claimed the position of authority among evangelicals."[23] This was seen in the surging popularity of integrated Christian counseling clinics such as Minirth-Meier, Ralpha, and New Life Treatment Centers. The integrated approach was further championed on the radio by organizations like Focus on the Family and by popular books by authors like Larry Crabb and Gary Collins.

The future seemed bleak for the BCM and the church as a whole seemed to have abandoned the sufficiency of Scripture to help God's people in exchange for the wisdom of man. However, God was still at work,

---

[22] Powlison, *The Biblical Counseling Movement*, 65.

[23] J. Cameron Fraser, *Developments in Biblical Counseling* (Grand Rapids, MI: Reformation Heritage Books, 2015), 7.

and he used a lawsuit to rekindle the nearly extinguished flame of the BCM.

THE LAWSUIT HEARD AROUND THE BIBLICAL COUNSELING WORLD

In 1979, a member of Grace Community Church in Sun Valley, California tragically committed suicide with a firearm.[24] He had a history of previous suicide attempts and had a handful of counseling/discipleship sessions with a pastor from the church. He was also evaluated by healthcare professionals for depression during the same period.

The man's family filed a lawsuit against Grace Community Church, Pastor John MacArthur, and three other pastors for "clergy malpractice and negligence and outrageous conduct in failing to prevent the suicide."[25] After a lengthy court battle, the church and its pastors were cleared of any wrongdoing. The lawsuit awoke a sleeping giant and Master's University and Seminary, the institutions associated with Grace Community Church quickly became one of the most outspoken supporters of biblical counseling.

The college replaced its psychology department with a biblical counseling department, organized by FBCM's Bob Smith, and then headed by CCEF's Wayne Mack; the church reorganized its large counseling

---

[24] 1988, "Just-IA US Law: Nally vs Grace Community Church," *JUSTIA*, https://law.justia.com/cases/california/supreme-court/3d/47/278.html.

[25] Ibid.

ministry along nouthetic counseling lines, and its pastors became certified with NANC.[26]

When the lawsuit was finally settled approximately a decade later, it had rejuvenated the interest and commitment that many churches and organizations had to biblical counseling.

ATTACKS FROM WITHIN THE MOVEMENT

The BCM has not just had to deal with attacks from the outside, but it has also had to deal with attacks from within the movement as well. Martin and Deirdre Bobgan were involved in the BCM in the late sixties and early seventies. By their own admission, they began a counseling ministry, trained others to be biblical counselors, and encouraged churches to have their own biblical counseling ministries.[27]

Over the years the Bogans became concerned that secular psychology was strongly influencing the BCM. As evidence, they cited the use of language such as "counselee," the invocation of titles such as "counselor," and the use of intake forms. They also were concerned that the BCM was becoming too problem-centered. When discussing problem-centered counseling, they stated, "What some who counsel may not realize is that it is entirely unnecessary to use a manual or even to discuss the problem that led the person to seek counsel."[28] As a

---

[26] Powlison, *The Biblical Counseling Movement*, 220.

[27] Martin and Deirdre Bogan, *Against the Biblical Counseling: FOR the Bible* (Santa Barbara, CA: EastGate Publishers, 1994), 167. See pp. 28-44 for a critical evaluation of the Bobgans material.

[28] Ibid., 13.

result of their concerns, the Bogans publicly stated in 1994, "We are so concerned that we are no longer recommending any biblical counseling centers or biblical counseling training."[29]

While the Bogans are relatively unknown to most Christians, they have heavily influenced the counseling approach of some popular Reformed pastors such as Peter Masters who is the current pastor of the Metropolitan Tabernacle in London, the pulpit that was made famous by Charles Spurgeon. The Bogans have taught at the Metropolitan Tabernacle on at least one occasion, and their influence can be seen in pastors who only counsel through preaching and neglect the private ministry of the Word. This has led to some pastors merely relying upon the doctrine of regeneration while neglecting to call believers to actively mortify specific sins.

THE STATE OF THE CURRENT BIBLICAL COUNSELING MOVEMENT

The BCM has seen an explosion in growth over the past few years. Its popularity has reached levels that its founders prayed for many years ago; God is clearly at work. ACBC has become the most prestigious and well respected certifying agency within the BCM. They recently announced their new record numbers at their 2019 Annual Conference. There are now nearly 2,000 certified members and over 70 ACBC certified training

---

[29] Ibid., 14.

centers.[30] ACBC noted that they are receiving record numbers of applications and inquiries from people considering certification.

The Institute of Nouthetic Studies (INS) was founded to promote the teachings of Adams and to allow students to learn directly from him through on-line courses. Recently, Mid-America Baptist Theological Seminary (MABTS) and INS entered into a partnership to provide biblical counseling training to its students and to offer accredited biblical counseling degrees. Another exciting aspect of the new partnership is that most of Adams' books will once again be available. A large number of his books had gone out of print when his previous publisher closed due to the death of its owner. Multiple seminaries, such as Southern Baptist Theological Seminary and Master's Seminary, offer advanced degrees in biblical counseling. Other seminaries have started to move in the direction of promoting biblical counseling instead of teaching an integrated model. For example, the Reformed Theological Seminary in Charlotte recently hired Jim Newheiser, a long-time supporter and practitioner of biblical counseling, to help revamp its counseling program.

Advancements in Biblical Counseling

Adams laid a firm foundation for the BCM in a very hostile and barren environment. Lambert has rightly noted that "Adams built a movement from scratch, almost

---

[30] Dale Johnson, *Association of Certified Biblical Counselor's Annual Conference* (Memphis, TN: Lecture, 2019).

alone, and was doing so against powerful forces opposed to his model."[31] Many faithful counselors built upon the sturdy foundation that Adams laid. Three of these advancements are an emphasis on the counselee as sufferer, a better understanding of motivation, and a less authoritative approach to counseling.[32]

The first advancement was a new emphasis on seeing counselees as a people who are suffering. Adams' methodology focused on recognizing sinful habit patterns in a counselee, confronting them, and replacing them with godly behaviors through the power of the Holy Spirit. In his methodology, a counselor did not spend a significant amount of time empathizing with a counselee. Adams did write about showing love and compassion to counselees, but it was not a major focus of his work. Lambert wrote:

> Counselees can find in Adams a counselor who understands the biblical theme of sin and who knows how to rebuke, confront, exhort, and point the way to biblical change. Not so apparent in Adams' style is a counselor who can identify with the sins and struggles of a counselee.[33]

Leaders in the BCM, such as Powlison, Lambert, and Newheiser, have advocated a methodology that encourages counselors to address a counselee's suffering

---

[31] Lambert, *The Biblical Counseling Movement After Adams*, 47.

[32] The Biblical Counseling Movement has experienced far more than three advancement in its theological practice, but only three will be examined in this chapter.

[33] Ibid., 96.

before confronting his sin. In so doing, biblical counselors seek to earn a counselee's trust through a more empathetic approach before offering rebuke and correction. For example, a counselor will spend some time addressing the pain and suffering that resulted from the sinful behavior before addressing the sin itself while never condoning it. The advancement of addressing suffering before sin is an improvement over Adams' methodology to some degree, but it can be an overcorrection if not properly practiced. Unfortunately, some counselors have taken this development to an extreme and have given what amounts to an excuse for sin.

The second advancement in the BCM has been a more expanded view on a counselee's motivation when it comes to sinful behavior. Adams strongly believed that sin is the primary reason that people behave the way that they do;[34] therefore, his counseling model is based upon changing the sinful habit patterns that a counselee has developed. He taught that change involved a "dehabituation and a rehabituation" process where counselees "put off" a sinful behavior or thought and "put on" a godly behavior or thought in its place. The put-off/put-on process is based upon Ephesians 4:17-24.

Mostly due to the influence of Powlison, the BCM eventually moved away from Adam's approach and towards one that had much more in common with the writings of the Puritans. Lambert explained that "For Powlison, the key that unlocks the door to motivation is worship. It is worship that motivates human activity. The

---

[34] Lambert, *The Biblical Counseling Movement After Adams*, 67.

central figure here is not whether there is worship, but instead what is being worshipped."[35] In other words, a person is either going to have God on the throne of his life or he will have something else instead. This approach attempts to identify and dethrone the idols in a person's heart.

The return to a more puritanical approach to counseling was a much-needed improvement. However, Adams' emphasis on the put-off/put-on process should not be disregarded since it is an intrinsic part of the biblical process of change. This process ought to be smoothly incorporated into the "Idols of the Heart" methodology of the later leaders in the BCM.

A third advancement in the BCM is a methodology that is more familial and less authoritarian in shape. Adams' focus was strongly based upon the shepherd/sheep relationship and he strongly believed that all counseling must be done in a formal setting. Lambert noted that "Adams's emphasis on pastoral authority tended to obscure the importance of building loving relationships with counselees."[36] Adams' formalized authoritarian methodology created some barriers to developing relationships in counseling. Despite Adams stressing the importance of providing loving and compassionate care to counselees, his approach has led to accusations that his methodology advocates an unloving and cruel approach.

As the movement has developed other leaders like Powlison and Mack have taken a different approach

---

[35] Ibid., 75.
[36] Ibid., 88.

that is still faithful to a model that recognizes the importance of authority in counseling; however, they take a more familial tone. They believe that often the most effective counseling is done when each party recognizes that the counselor is also a sinner saved by grace. They take the approach that counseling can often be done in a more informal setting. According to Lambert:

> The counselor does possess the authority of God when speaking from God's Word. When, however, the counselor speaks the Word to a counselee, he or she is speaking to a brother or sister in Christ. The counselor is still speaking authoritatively, but authority has a different tone when done in the context of a brother-sister relationship than when it is done in a general-corporal relationship.[37]

While less of an emphasis on formalized, authoritarian counseling has been a much-needed advancement, the BCM must not throw the baby out with the bathwater. There is still a place for formalized counseling sessions that are authoritarian in nature, but this approach should not automatically be the default methodology.

Areas in Need of Advancement

While the BCM has made great advancements over the last few decades, there are still several areas that are in need of improvement. Due to length constraints,

---

[37] Ibid., 91.

only three areas will be briefly discussed.

The first area in need of advancement is the recognition of the role that the doctrines of grace play in the presuppositions and the practices of counselors. Adams felt that this topic was very important, but it is completely neglected in biblical counseling literature.[38] Unfortunately, Adams only addressed the topic in a small twenty-page booklet called *Counseling and the Five Points of Calvinism.* Further work is needed to emphasize that a firm understanding of the five points of Calvinism and the sovereignty of God are fundamental in providing biblical counsel.

A second area in need of advancement is determining how to better provide biblical counsel to people in the midst of a crisis. Serious suicidal threats and the unexpected death of a child are just two examples of realistic situations wherein biblical counseling resources are lacking. Adams said that "Each minister of the Word, during the course of his ministry, must help others to face the many crises that unavoidably arise in a sinful world."[39] A vast majority of the current biblical counseling resources help equip pastors and counselors to care for people in controlled environments over a period of time. There are only a few biblical counseling resources available that tackle the tough topic of how to counsel someone in a life-changing crisis when you do not have the luxury of time or a controlled environment. The

---

[38] Jay Adams, *Counseling and the Five Points of Calvinism* (Phillipsburg, NJ: Presbyterian and Reformed Publishing Company, 1981), 7.

[39] Jay Adams. *Coping with Counseling Crises* (Grand Rapids, MI: Baker Book House Company, 1976), 1.

resources that do exist mostly teach an integrated approach. There is a desperate need for more resources to assist counselors; especially for those who serve as chaplains.

A third area in need of advancement is the development of a biblical approach for people who are suffering from Post-Traumatic Stress Disorder (PTSD). The secular world has long recognized the long-term damaging effects brought about by experiencing or witnessing a traumatic event. Secularists have developed treatment plans for people suffering from PTSD that are often grossly unbiblical. Unfortunately, the BCM has been very slow in recognizing PTSD and in developing biblical solutions. While there have been some small advancements in this area through the work of counselors like Daniel Berger, the need for work in this area seems to be growing exponentially.

THREATS TO THE BIBLICAL COUNSELING MOVEMENT

The BCM is currently experiencing a surge of popularity and acceptance however, there are dangers that threaten to curtail the movement and steer it toward unbiblical methods. The following are four threats that the BCM must recognize and address biblically.

The first threat to the BCM is the massive neglect of hermeneutical training in a majority of non-college/seminary based biblical counseling training courses. Many training centers do a good job of covering the sufficiency of Scripture and how to generically counsel specific problems. Unfortunately, very little to no time is spent on how to interpret the Bible in its appropriate context and how to apply it outside of a cookie-cutter approach. As a result, many Christians who complete a training course are ill-equipped to correctly apply Scripture to difficult and unusual situations. To defend against this threat, the BCM must insist on the inclusion of hermeneutical training in all training courses.

The second threat to the BCM is the overemphasis that has been placed on biblical counseling certifications and biblical counseling degrees. This emphasis is inadvertently creating a special class of pastors and counselors. The proliferation of graduate and doctoral degrees in biblical counseling from respectable Christian institutions is a good sign and should be encouraged. However, this proliferation has unintended consequences. It has inadvertently caused some people to seek help from outside of their local church because they think that their pastor is ill-equipped and unable to counsel them if they do not have a biblical counseling degree or certification. To defend against this threat, the BCM needs to stress that a pastor who does not have a high-end degree or certification is still competent to counsel.

The third threat to the BCM is an abandonment of the work of Adams in much of the modern BCM. Many training courses do not require its students to read any of his books and may not even mention his name with the exception of mentioning areas that they feel that he fell short. There are some great training programs at places like Master's Seminary, MABTS, and INS that continue to promote and emphasize the importance of Adams' works, but sadly they are in the minority.

Just like any other theologian, Adams was not perfect. However, his insights into how to care for the souls of man and his boldness in proclaiming the sufficiency of Scripture is something that all biblical counselors can learn from. If the BCM neglects to read and study its foundational books such as *Competent to Counsel,* it sets itself up to fall into the same errors that led to the infestation of psychology into the counseling of God's people.

The fourth threat to the BCM is the name biblical counseling. Many Christian counselors refer to what they do as biblical counseling, even though it is vastly different from the methodology of the BCM. For example, 'deliverance ministers' who focus on "casting out demons" as a means of sanctification often refer to themselves as biblical counselors. Also, many integrated Christian counselors whose methodology is based upon a Christianized version of psychology also refer to themselves as biblical counselors. When biblical counselors were referred to as "Nouthetic Counselors" it clearly distinguished them from these other types of biblical counselors. When NANC changed their name to ACBC, it basically caused the entire movement to stop referring to their methodology as "nouthetic" and to start using the generic word "biblical." While it solved the problem of having to explain what the word nouthetic meant, it simultaneously caused an identity issue. To defend against this threat, the BCM must find a way to clearly distinguish itself from other types of so-called biblical counseling.

The fifth threat to the BCM is the current political climate in the United States. There is a growing tide within society that is turning against biblical principles. State licensed counselors risk losing their license if they witness to a counselee unless the topic is brought up by a counselee and prohibit them from addressing specific sin issues that society wholeheartedly embraces. While these laws currently do not affect non-licensed church-based counselors, it may only be a matter of time. As the culture becomes more hostile to Christianity, it will attempt to stop the church from teaching and practicing beliefs that it finds to be intolerant. This is likely to include what is said in the counseling room.

CONCLUSION

Church history has shown us that God will raise up the right man at the right time to accomplish His goals. In the case of the BCM, that man was Adams. Over the last fifty years, we have seen God's providential hand throughout the BCM. At times it faltered and even swayed from the path, but it always returned at the call of the Shepherd's voice. While many challenges lay ahead, the movement is standing on a firm foundation. I pray that God will raise up other fearless warriors to stand on the truth of the sufficiency of Scripture for counseling.

2

A Critical Evaluation of the Anti-Biblical Counseling Movement

Michael R. Burgos

At nearly fifty years old, the biblical counseling movement (BCM) has given most of its attention to both internal developments via continual reformation to the biblical text and its ongoing turf war with secular psychology and the integrationist movement. However, there exists another interlocutor, namely the anti-biblical counseling movement (A-BCM) as it exists among conservative Protestants who simultaneously reject psychology and the resultant psychotherapies. This movement, beginning in the late 1980s,[40] has received little attention from within the BCM, likely due to its small size and somewhat incendiary approach. Despite any attention the A-BCM received in the early 1990s, it is virtually now ignored by the BCM.

The leaders and most vocal advocates of the A-BCM are Martin and Deidre Bobgan. Martin Bobgan has a doctoral degree in educational psychology, and he and his wife have produced a substantial number of books and articles which seek to refute the existence of the BCM on biblical and theological grounds. The Bobgans were initially supportive of the BCM, even collaborating with Adams on several projects.[41] That support was withdrawn and the Bobgans began to attack the BCM continually.[42] Despite the A-BCM's attempts, the BCM has enjoyed considerable success within many churches and institutions. However, the A-BCM has made some inroads into several notable churches and ministries. For instance, Martin Bobgan spoke against biblical counseling at C. H. Spurgeon's own, Metropolitan

---

[40] David Powlison, *The Biblical Counseling Movement: History and Context* (Greensboro, NC: New Growth Press, 2010), 217-8.

[41] E.g., Martin & Deidre Bobgan eds., *Prophets of Psychoheresy I* (Santa Barbara, CA: EastGate Pub., 1989).

[42] E.g., Martin & Deidre Bobgan, *Competent to Minister: The Biblical Care of Souls* (Santa Barbara, CA: EastGate Pub., 1996); *Against Biblical Counseling: FOR the Bible* (Santa Barbara, CA: EastGate Pub., 1994); *Stop Counseling! Start Ministering!* (Santa Barbara, CA: EastGate Pub., 2011); *Counseling the Hard Cases: A Critical Review* (Santa Barbara, CA: EastGate Pub., 2016).

Tabernacle in London.[43] Additionally, the Berean Call, the ministry started by the late Dave Hunt, has continued to promote the Bobgans A-BCM materials.[44]

While the Bobgan's book entitled *Against Biblical Counseling: FOR the Bible* is one of many texts which voice opposition to the BCM, this text articulates all of the major arguments of the A-BCM in a single volume. This chapter will interact with those arguments presented in *Against the Biblical Counseling*, demonstrating that the A-BCM's major objections are unfounded and predicated upon faulty logic and, in some cases, legalism.[45]

AN EVALUATION OF A-BCM OBJECTIONS

The A-BCM has raised a series of objections that strike at the very heart of the BCM. Below I have provided a summarization of each main objection followed by my critical evaluation.

---

[43] Martin & Deidre Bobgan, *A Church's Unholy Alliance with the Four Temperaments* (Santa Barbara, CA: EastGate Pub., 1992), 2. Cf. Johnson who wrote, "They [i.e., the Bobgans] appear to relatively little influence outside of a small group of like-minded extremists." Eric L. Johnson, *Foundations of Christian Soul Care* (Downers Grove, IL: IVP Academic, 2007), 111.

[44] E.g., Martin & Deidra Bobgan, 06/01/2004, "Christ-Centered Ministry Vs. Problem Centered Counseling," The Berean Call, https://www.thebereancall.org/content/june-2014-extra-bobgan.

[45] By "legalism" I am not here referring to soteriological legalism but the adoption of prohibitions that are not found in Scripture. These extra-biblical prohibitions violate the principle of 1 Cor. 4:6 wherein Paul instructed the Corinthians "learn by us not to go beyond what is written."

Summary of Objection I: Biblical Counseling is Integrationism

Biblical counselors teach a novel form of "psychoheresy" (i.e., psychology) "by using the unproved and unscientific psychological opinions of men."[46] Namely, biblical counselors engage in the same self-focused method of secular psychologies.[47] Biblical counselors focus on problems and not sanctification. "Biblical counselors too often attempt to solve problems at the surface level, or they attempt to discover something about the inner man through various methods of exploration."[48] The counselor-counselee paradigm is unbiblical and derived from the secular therapeutic culture, and sets the counselor up as an expert.[49] One to one counseling is unbiblical and also a takeover from secular therapy. Charging for counseling is unbiblical and illegitimate.[50]

A Response to Objection I

The BCM originated as a theologically conservative and Calvinistic project which sought to recover the ecclesiastical and institutional ground taken by an influx of secular therapeutic practitioners within conservative evangelicalism.[51] The BCM waged a

---

[46] Bobgan, *Against Biblical Counseling*, 100.

[47] Ibid., 19.

[48] Ibid., 20.

[49] Ibid., 19, 75, 82, 91.

[50] Ibid., 88-9.

[51] Powlison, *The Biblical Counseling Movement*, 40-1, 51.

"jurisdictional conflict"[52] with psychology and psychiatry, as these disciplines encroached upon territory formally occupied by those who recognized the Bible to be the sufficient means of instruction for Christian soul care. This was a movement that sought to recover the heart and soul of the inerrantist church through theological polemics and the recovery of a positive model of counseling derived from Scripture.[53]

While conservative Protestantism had focused its efforts upon defeating the threats of modernity, it had failed to adequately answer the psychological revolution of the post-civil war era.[54] This period brought with it a terrific need for biblical soul care. Instead of meeting the needs of the public with a robust practical theology, the church effectively handed over the responsibility of its soul care to the new "science" of psychology.[55] In the aftermath of the great wars of the twentieth century, psychology had solidified its place within the church. The BCM, taking its cues from its Reformation heritage, sought to reform the church's understanding of

---

[52] Ibid., 1-2, 15.

[53] The initial polemic work was Jay E. Adams, *Competent to Counsel: Introduction to Nouthetic Counseling* (Grand Rapids, MI: Zondervan, 1970), and continues with recent efforts such as Powlison's work in Eric L. Johnson ed., *Psychology and Christianity: Five Views*, 2nd Ed. (Downers Grove, IL: IVP Academic, 2010).

[54] Heath Lambert, *The Biblical Counseling Movement After Adams* (Wheaton, IL: Crossway, 2012), 34-5.

[55] There exists significant reason to doubt the credibility of psychology as a legitimate science given its inability to follow standard scientific procedures. See pp. 64-75.

counseling back to the teaching of Scripture; effectively dislodging psychology from its place within evangelicalism.

Biblical counseling is the practical and timely application of the Bible's teaching to the life of someone who has problems, questions, or some kind of trouble.[56] Biblical counseling is not the proclamation of the facts of the Christian faith in the abstract, but the particular application of biblical truth to specific events, persons, and things.[57] Therefore, biblical counseling has existed long before what we know today as the BCM. What Adams began in the 1970s was merely a *return* to the cure of souls that had been a fixture within the church for millennia. That the BCM wasn't innovating may be seen in its dependence upon the soul care of English-speaking puritanism, the reformers, and even the patristic writers.[58]

---

[56] Heath Lambert, *A Theology of Biblical Counseling: The Doctrinal Foundations of Counseling Ministry* (Grand Rapids, MI: Zondervan, 2016), 13.

[57] Some critics of the BCM have wrongly characterized it in reductionistic terms, claiming that biblical counseling is about merely identifying sin and giving the counselee a few Bible lessons. E.g., Darlene Parsons, 12/15/2017, "Biblical Counseling Training: Inadequate Education, Problematic Resources and Questionably Educated Leaders," *The Wartburg Watch*, http://thewartburgwatch.com/2017/12/15/biblical-counseling-training-inadequate-education-problematic-resources-and-questionably-educated-leaders/. Cf. Kathryn Joyce, 06/14/2017, "The Rise of Biblical Counseling," *Pacific Standard*, https://psmag.com/social-justice/evangelical-prayer-bible-religion-born-again-christianity-rise-biblical-counseling-89464.

[58] Mark A. Deckard, *Helpful Truth in Past Places: The Puritan Practice of Biblical Counseling* (Fearn, UK:

Hence, any claim that the BCM is merely a twentieth-century novelty, or that it is contrary to the church's tradition of soul care is misguided and dependent upon a mischaracterization of the BCM from the outset.

The theological and methodological vision laid by Adams in the 1970s has been built upon, refined, and even corrected by the BCM itself.[59] Although much development and reformation continues in the third generation of the BCM, the presuppositions and general principles of the movement have remained unchanged. At its root, the fundamental presupposition of the BCM is a theocentric worldview expressed in the historic Reformed faith and its commitment to a high view of the Triune God. Unlike liberal Protestantism, with its subjugation of biblical revelation to the acids of modernity, or the modern therapeutic culture, which founds its

---

Mentor, 2010); Fraser, *Developments in Biblical Counseling*, 91-107; T. Dale Johnson, "A Case for Religious Liberty in Soul Care From a Historical Perspective," *The Journal for Biblical Soul Care*, 1.1, 34-55; Timothy J. Keller, 1988, "Puritan Resources for Biblical Counseling," *Journal of Pastoral Practice*, 9.3, 11-44; Jeremy Lelek, *Biblical Counseling Basics: Roots, Beliefs, Future* (Greensboro, NC: New Growth Press, 2018), 9-11; John F. MacArthur et al., *Introduction to Biblical Counseling* (Dallas, TX: Word Pub., 1994), 21-43; David Powlison, 2008, "Looking at the Past and Present of Counseling," *9Marks Journal*, 5.6, 18-21; Cf. John Weaver, *The Failure of Evangelical Mental Health Care: Treatments That Harm Women, LGBT Persons, and the Mentally Ill* (Jefferson, NC: McFarland & Co., 2015), 20.

[59] Lambert, *The Biblical Counseling Movement After Adams*, 87-138 and J. Cameron Fraser, *Developments in Biblical Counseling* (Reformation Heritage Books, 2015), 59-90.

presuppositions on the transient ground of moral individualism, Reformed Protestantism has received the canon of Scripture as the *only* sufficient and infallible rule of Christian faith and practice. As a product of Reformed thought, the BCM has always been predicated upon the reformation principle of *Sola Scriptura*.[60] Thus, from its inception, the BCM has sought to make the contents of its counseling biblical.

Given this presupposition, biblical counselors seek to address the issues of their counselees using a theological lexicon and a biblical worldview. The content of biblical counseling is Scripture and its shape imperatival. While there is a time for listening and the gathering of information regarding a situation, biblical counseling is directive, giving concrete applications of biblical truth to a person's life. Thus, the notion that biblical counseling is "self-focused" is an inexcusable mischaracterization. Not only can one survey the literature published by biblical counselors in the last fifty years and see that this assertion is untrue, but even the most cursory examination of the BCM refutes such a claim.

The Bobgans claim that the biblical counselors focus on "problems and not sanctification," and that biblical counselors have baptized the problem-centered approach of psychotherapy. This objection is curious since there are numerous apostolic examples of problem-

---

[60] For a concise articulation of the sufficiency of Scripture as it relates to counseling see Wayne A. Mack, 1998, "The Sufficiency of Scripture in Counseling," *TMSJ*, 9.1, 63-84.

focused counsel. The apostle Paul spent the first four chapters of 1 Corinthians writing about his reader's problems, but he was simultaneously focusing upon sanctification. Hence, it is a false dichotomy to suppose that focusing on peoples' problems is contrary to sanctification. Moreover, even if one were to ignore the biblical examples, it would be a genetic fallacy to suppose that since psychotherapy utilizes a problem-centered model, it is therefore wrong.[61] Addressing someone's pornography addiction through the specific application of the Bible's teaching on lust and idolatry is not "surface level" problem-solving. Applying the Psalms to the heart of the depressed such that they find solace in communion with God is not superficial problem-solving. Rather, biblical counseling is always imperatival and has sanctification as its goal.[62]

Because of the existence of the counselor-counselee paradigm, the Bobgans have accused the BCM of integrationism. To these charges, it must first be observed that the Bobgans have gone beyond what is

---

[61] For a concise explanation of the genetic fallacy see Richard A. Holland Jr., Benjamin K. Forrest, *Good Arguments: Making Your Case in Writing and Public Speaking* (Grand Rapids, MI: Baker, 2017), 43.

[62] Adams wrote, "Biblical change is the goal of counseling." Jay E. Adams, *A Theology of Christian Counseling: More Than Redemption* (Grand Rapids, MI: Zondervan, 1979), 234. See also Lambert, A Theology of Biblical Counseling, 292; Robert W. Kellemen, *Gospel-Centered Counseling: How Christ Changes Lives* (Grand Rapids, MI: Zondervan, 2014), 260; and Stuart Scott's work in Stephen P. Greggo, Timothy A. Sisemore eds., *Counseling and Christianity: Five Approaches* (Downers Grove, IL: IVP Academic, 2012), 167-70.

written in Scripture to make these arguments (1 Cor. 4:6). There is no text prohibiting the use of "counselor" language. Rather, the language of "counselor" and "counselee" reflects a biblical category of function among God's people. Scripture depicts those who give wise counsel as a great asset (Prov. 11:14; 20:18; 24:6) and the apostle Paul engaged in one on one counseling among the believers in Ephesus (Acts 20:20, v. 31; cf. Rom. 15:14; Col. 1:28).

Second, the notion that biblical counselors are assumed to be experts by all who seek their counsel is misguided. Rather, one seeks the aid of a counselor because he believes that the counselor has wisdom sufficient for the task. A Christian who struggles with doubt wouldn't likely seek the counsel of a new believer, but one who is mature and who has weathered the affliction of this life and is yet faithful. While upholding the importance of ordained churchmen as especially responsible for counseling, the BCM has *always* asserted the need for every believer to become a biblical counselor.[63]

The rationale one would use in order to sell a book on the subject of counseling to Christians is the same rationale one would use in charging a fee for counseling. The Scripture warns of those who peddle God's truth for a profit (2 Cor. 2:17) but it does not prohibit either Christian writers, ministers, teachers, or those whose vocation is counseling from charging a fee for their labor.

---

[63] Jay E. Adams, *The Christian Counselor's Manual* (Grand Rapids, MI: Zondervan, 1973), 9.

The apostle Paul gave a specific justification of earning a living from the ministry in 1 Corinthians 9:1-18. In this pericope, Paul sought to exemplify the doctrine of Christian liberty. In their earlier correspondence, the Corinthian church had questioned Paul regarding eating meat offered to pagan idols.[64] Within the relevant era in Corinth, most butcheries incorporated a token pagan ritual and therefore a diet of meat generally connoted an assent to paganism.[65] Recent converts, having been introduced into an entirely exclusive theology wherein the Triune God is the only suitable object of devotion and worship, would have naturally struggled with parsing through whether eating meat was tantamount to a return to their old way of life. Paul addresses this issue by recognizing that "idols are nothing in the world" (8:4), and that believers are free to eat meat, but must temper their liberty when around those whose consciences are weak. It is on the heels of this discussion that Paul gives an illustration of this principle. In 1 Corinthians 9:4-5, Paul noted that in the same way one has the freedom to eat or drink or to take a wife, those in the ministry have a "right" (Gk. *exousia*) to earn their living from the ministry. In the case of the church in Corinth, Paul chose not to exercise this right for strategic reasons (vv. 12-13). It is certain,

---

[64] 1 Cor. 8:1. The abruptness of the introduction *peri de tōn eidōlothutōn* ("Now concerning meat sacrificed to idols") implies that this topic was one that was featured in the Corinthian correspondence to Paul (cf. 1 Cor. 7:1).

[65] Alex T. Cheung, *Idol Food in Corinth: Jewish Background and Pauline Legacy* (Sheffield, UK: Sheffiled Academic Press, 1999), 35-8. See also Khiok-khng Yeo, *Rhetorical Interaction in 1 Corinthians 8 and 10* (Leiden, NL: Brill, 1995), 95-101.

however, that Paul did receive payment from other churches (Phil. 4:16-18; cf. Gal. 6:6; 1 Tim. 5:8). Thus, we may discern from Paul's example that charging for work in the ministry is up to the liberty of the individual believer and his conscience.[66] It is legalism to assert, as the Bobgans do, that it is unlawful or unbiblical to charge for biblical counseling.

Summary of Objection II: Specialized Education in Biblical Counseling Unnecessary & Unbiblical

The BCM movement is guilty of making pastors feel intimidated because of a lack of specialized training in biblical counseling.[67] The Bobgans reject the notion that any specialized education should be offered for those who are seeking to become equipped to engage in counseling. If pastors 100-300 years ago could "preach the Gospel and teach the Word concerning the on-going walk of the believer in sanctification," and they didn't have specialized education, no one needs such training today. Biblical counseling training serves to intimidate pastors, making them feel inadequate for ministry.

A Response to Objection II

As previously noted, the BCM is a resurgent movement that has sought to recapture the ecclesiastical and institutional ground taken by psychology and

---

[66] This view is also reflected in the Association of Certified Biblical Counselors *Standards of Conduct* § III.C. See 10/04/2016, "Standards of Conduct," *Association of Certified Biblical Counselors,* https://biblicalcounseling.com/certification/standards-of-conduct/.

[67] Bobgan, *Against Biblical Counseling,* 11.

psychiatry practitioners. An examination of conservative Bible colleges and seminaries demonstrates that most do not teach the sufficiency of Scripture for soul care, but the necessity of secular theories and the accompanying methodologies. Hence, there is a great need for a return to the all-sufficient resources of Scripture for soul care, and that is precisely what the BCM has sought over the length of its existence.

It is only within the context of a dearth of true practical theology that one can describe biblical counseling training as "specialized." Most seminary training focuses its curriculum upon the public ministry of the Word through teaching and preaching, but very little on the private ministry of the Word (i.e., counseling) (Eph. 4:11-16). "The typical seminary curriculum has just one counseling class in 100-credit-hour master of divinity degree."[68] It is a mischaracterization to assert that the BCM is attempting to add some new form of training otherwise unknown to seminarians.[69] Rather, biblical counseling training a return to biblical theology for Christian soul care. Furthermore, it is more likely that any pastoral intimidation is due to a lack of fluency with psychological diagnoses given the culture's slavish devotion to the psychotherapeutic establishment. Biblical

---

[68] Bob Kellemen, Kevin Carson eds., *Biblical Counseling and the Church: God's Care Through God's People* (Grand Rapids, MI: Zondervan, 2015), 34.

[69] Welch, referring to the Christian gospel and the Scriptures, has suggested that intimidated pastors "Already know the most helpful truths" See Edward T. Welch, 12/17/2018, "Five Encouragements for Pastors Intimidated by Biblical Counseling," *9Marks*, https://www.9marks.org/article/intimidated/.

counseling effectively demystifies the psychological lexicon, viewing human problems through a biblical framework.[70] Even if one were to grant that biblical counseling training is some sort of specialty, there is no biblical text which prohibits one from gaining extraordinary knowledge in the care of souls.

Summary of Objection III: Parachurch Counseling Centers and Counseling Ministries Within Churches Are Unbiblical

Any "biblical counseling ministries that operate outside the church, those that function as separate entities inside churches, and all organizations that train biblical counselors for ministries that are visibly separated from the biblically ordained ministries of the Church"[71] are unnecessary and unbiblical. "A step forward for those in the biblical counseling movement would be to discontinue all biblical counseling centers that operate outside of a church."[72]

A Response to Objection III

From its inception to the present day, the BCM has stressed the need for the local church to be the means

---

[70] An excellent example of this is Michael R. Emlet, *Descriptions and Prescriptions: A Biblical Perspective on Psychiatric Diagnoses & Medications* (Greensboro, NC: New Growth Press, 2017).

[71] Bobgan, *Against Biblical Counseling*, 58.

[72] Ibid., 90; cf. 71, 94.

of meeting the counseling needs of believers.[73] The BCM has never been a movement that has emphasized any form of ministry outside of the local church. Adam's initial model of biblical counseling affirmed the need for every believer to counsel[74] but emphasized the ordained minister as the quintessential counselor of God's people.[75] Of Romans 15:14, Adams wrote, "Paul recognized that any Christian may engage in nouthetic counseling, so long as he possesses the qualities of goodness and knowledge."[76] The BCM has always recognized that "The authority for counseling is granted through Christ's Church."[77] One can see the BCM's commitment to the supremacy of the local church in its correlation of biblical counseling and church discipline.[78]

The presupposition underlying the Bobgan's rejection of any parachurch counseling organization is a rigid definition of the church that is itself unbiblical. When the Bobgans say "discontinue all biblical counseling centers that operate outside of a church," they are implying that "church" means what Christians do in a building on Sunday and other worship times. This

---

[73] Kellemen et al., *Biblical Counseling and the Church*, 184-5. David Powlison, 2014, "The Local Church is THE Place for Biblical Counseling," *CCEF Now*, 2-3.

[74] Adams, Competent to Counsel, 41-2.

[75] Ibid., 65-7;

[76] Ibid., 60.

[77] Adams, *A Theology of Christian Counseling*, 279. See also MacArthur et al., *Introduction to Biblical Counseling*, 301-10; Paul David Tripp, *Instruments in the Redeemer's Hands* (Phillipsburg, NJ: P & R, 2002), *esp.* 18ff;

[78] E.g., Adams, *A Theology of Christian Counseling*, 278-80.

definition, however, is too narrow to be biblical. While the Scriptures do use the term "church" to speak of a local fellowship (Rom. 16:5), the Bible also speaks of the church in provincial terms (Acts 9:31), and even the church catholic (1 Cor. 15:9). Powlison and Lambert note that "The diverse use of the term *church* in the Bible provides a strong biblical justification within which Christians may organize themselves to serve in activities we call parachurch."[79]

The local church is clearly the focus of the redemptive efforts of the Triune God on earth, and therefore, parachurch ministries should serve at the pleasure and for the good of the local church. Parachurch ministries that either compete with the church or are completely outside local church authority are indeed unbiblical. However, if a parachurch organization exists to serve and complement the local church and its mission, its ministry is legitimate:

> The centrality of the local church congregation is actually an argument for principled parachurch ministry—so long as such ministries direct their energies toward the church's thriving. That is so for seminaries, prison ministries, and international missions societies. It is so for counseling ministries and every other form of faithful and useful parachurch organization.[80]

---

[79] David Powlison, Heath Lambert, 2019, "Biblical Counseling in Local Churches and Parachurch Ministries," *Journal of Biblical Counseling*, 33.2, 14-15.
[80] Ibid., 15.

The BCM has made use of parachurch ministries which recognize the supremacy of the local church. Biblical counseling parachurch ministries do not, as the Bobgan's have asserted, replace the local church. Ironically, the Bobgans run a parachurch organization (i.e., "PsychoHeresy Awareness Ministries"), and even implicitly support the role of other parachurch organizations such as seminaries.[81] It would stand to reason, therefore, if parachurch counseling ministries are unbiblical, then so are parachurch anti-counseling ministries. Additionally, there is no biblical imperative, whether explicit or implicit, that precludes the existence of parachurch counseling ministries. Hence, the Bobgan's objection to parachurch counseling is, like their objection to making a living from the ministry and the existence of biblical counseling training, predicated upon an extrabiblical prohibition.

CONCLUSION

It has been shown above that the three main objections raised by the anti-biblical counseling movement depend upon mischaracterizations of the BCM. So too, the A-BCM's objections to earning a living from counseling ministry, biblical counseling education, and the existence of parachurch counseling ministries go beyond what is written in Scripture, landing in bald legalism. Particularly in the case of earning a living from the ministry, there is a clear didactic text which has specifically precluded the Bobgan's objections.

---

[81] Bobgan, *Against Biblical Counseling*, 9, 187.

The BCM is founded upon the bulwark of biblical sufficiency and has ably sought to expand the vision first articulated by Adams to local churches throughout North America and beyond. It is a movement that, while undergoing continual reformation, remains committed to fidelity to the biblical text and the local church.

3

ON THE LOGIC OF THE BIBLICAL COUNSELING MOVEMENT & ACCREDITATION

Michael R. Burgos

A HOLY INSURGENCY

An insurgent movement seeks to invalidate and dethrone an established occupier. Insurgencies are almost always grassroots; a rebellion by everyday visionaries against systemic wrongdoing. From its inception, the biblical counseling movement has been a theological insurgency. It has sought to restore the church's understanding of counseling as an intrinsically theological task for which Scripture is sufficient. The biblical counseling movement has simultaneously sought to refute the psychotherapeutic establishment and integrationist counterinsurgency.

Key to the success of any insurgent movement is the establishment of new institutions that serve to herald and pursue the cause. In the case of the biblical counseling movement, many new institutions have been formed. These include accrediting bodies that have set ethical and theological standards for the practice of biblical counseling. Chief among these accrediting institutions is The Association of Certified Biblical Counselors (ACBC). By design, the certification ACBC offers is not recognized by any governmental agency. There is no sanctioning body that has granted validity to ACBC. Rather, ACBC looks to local churches and other Christian ministries to recognize its credibility. In so doing, ACBC has intentionally bucked the bureaucratic expectations of our culture. It has, upon the basis of the Lordship of King Jesus, set up shop *on biblical terms*. Whereas Licensed Professional Counselors, Licensed Mental Health Counselors, and others depend upon the state to approve their labor, ACBC and the biblical counseling movement have sought the approval of heaven.

The logic of ACBC (or any other biblical counseling certifying body) as an institution is clear. ACBC has effectively repudiated secular counseling accreditation as even relevant.[82] Just as the Lord's Supper and the public exposition of the Word of God resides within the jurisdiction of the local church, so does the cure of souls. There is neither a need nor a basis for

---

[82] See 2019, "Statement on Licensure," *Association of Certified Biblical Counselors*, https://biblicalcounseling.com/statement-on-licensure/.

governmental oversight or approval in these matters. Rather, the authority for ministry is bound up in the charter given by Christ to his people (Matt. 28:19).

HONOR THE LORD YOUR FAFSA…

Inasmuch as counseling is the prerogative of God's people, so is theological education and ministerial training. In our day, most who desire to enter into vocational ministry first attend either a Bible college or seminary (or both). This formalized training comes at a price, as the average MDiv costs upwards of $45,000.[83] Fortunately, most conservative seminaries accept federal student loans such that seminarians may become enslaved (Prov. 22:7) to the federal government just prior to entering the ministry.

Truly, the vast majority of conservative Protestant seminaries would not exist were it not for federal money. Those seminaries who reject Caesar's cash derive much of their funding from tax-exempt local churches—as it should be.[84] In order for a Bible college or seminary to lay claim to federal money, that school must become accredited by either a regional or national accreditor that is recognized by either the U. S.

---

[83] According to the Association of Theological Schools, the preeminent national accreditor for seminaries, the average tuition cost for MDiv students per year was $15,442 in 2018-19. Conventional MDiv programs are three years of graduate study (i.e., 90 credit hours). 2019, "2018 - 2019 Annual Data Tables," *Association of Theological Schools Commission on Accrediting*, 4.1. https://www.ats.edu/uploads/resources/institutional-data/annual-data-tables/2018-2019-annual-data-tables.pdf.

[84] E.g., The Southern Baptist Theological Seminary.

Department of Education (DOE) or Council for Higher Education Accreditation (CHEA).[85] So too, there are other reasons institutions seek accreditation. For example, recognized accreditation is a form of statist approval, without which an institution is generally considered illegitimate at best. Jamin Hübner has observed, "Higher-education in the 'developed' world, whether religious or not, tends to be arranged to favor education that is validated by a government."[86] Subsequently, "Accreditors generally function as an arm of the state."[87]

Accreditation says almost nothing about academic rigor, let alone an institution's fidelity to Scripture.[88] Consider Union Theological Seminary (UTS) in New York City. UTS has regional accreditation from the Middle States Commission on Higher Education, as

---

[85] There are other reasons institutions seek recognized accreditation, including the illegality in some states of operating an unaccredited institution of post-secondary education. For instance, in my home state of CT, there is not a religious exemption clause for a degree-granting non-accredited Bible institute or seminary.

[86] Jamin Hübner, 2017, "Obstacles to Change: Overcoming Hurdles of the State Apparatus in Higher Education," *Journal of Religious Leadership*, 16.1, 21. Walston wrote similarly, "Quite simply, accreditation is validation." Rick Walston, *Walston's Guide to Christian Distance Learning*, 5th Ed. (Maitland, FL: Xulon Press, 2007), 64. See also Susan D. Phillips, Kevin Kinser eds., *Accreditation on the Edge: Challenging Quality Assurance in Higher Education* (Baltimore, MD: Johns Hopkins Univ. Press, 2018), 233-4.

[87] Hübner, "Obstacles to Change," 22.

[88] This is true even of what is arguably the most evangelical of recognized accreditors, the Transnational Association of Christian Colleges and Schools.

well as national accreditation from the Association of Theological Schools. While UTS has the most prestigious accreditation possible, the education it affords is a morass of unbelief.

While most equate "accredited" with "legitimate," achieving accreditation merely reveals a school's conformity to the administrative and financial expectations of the accreditor, and by extension, the federal government. Recognized accreditation cannot answer the questions most students might ask of a Bible college or seminary: "Is the faculty faithful unto God?," "Is the curricula effective and God-honoring?," "Will I receive the best training here?" or "Will an education at this school prepare me for the mission field?"

Any doubt about government control through recognized accreditors should have evaporated when the New England Association of Schools and Colleges (NEASC) implied that Gordon College's policy on homosexual practice was out of step with its accreditation standards.[89] Another example can be seen in the treatment of the Master's University by one of its accreditors, the Western Association of Schools and Colleges (WASC). WASC has sought to enforce ethical standards and practices upon Master's,[90] just as with NEASC and

---

[89] David French, 2015, "Gordon College Keeps Its Faith and Its Accreditation," *National Review*, https://www.nationalreview.com/2015/05/gordon-college-keeps-its-faith-and-its-accreditation-david-french/.

[90] See WASC's action letter to Dr. John MacArthur (2018): https://wascsenior.box.com/shared/static/c6ojdrd8tt4w1le7it98nyag0z7d6gzb.pdf.

Gordon College. One would expect a Christian institution to form its ethical practices upon the basis of a biblically informed Christian worldview rather than the ephemeral mores of a regional accreditor.

Similar observations can be made in light of the treatment of two other evangelical institutions by recognized accreditors, namely, Patrick Henry College and Westminster Theological Seminary (Philadelphia). Patrick Henry College sought accreditation with the American Academy for Liberal Education and was denied because of its commitment to creationism.[91] The Middle States Association of Colleges and Schools (MSACS) threatened to revoke Westminster's accreditation in the 1990s because of a lack of women on its oversight board.[92] Westminster's charter requires its board to be comprised of ordained elders. MSACS rescinded its threat a year later when Westminster agreed "to give women a voice in its educational decision-making process."[93]

---

[91] Latonya Taylor, 07/08/2002, "Christian College Denied Accreditation," *Christianity Today*, https://www.christianitytoday.com/ct/2002/july8/15.16.html.

[92] 10/22/1990, "Seminary May Lose Accreditation," *Christianity Today*, https://www.christianitytoday.com/ct/1990/october-22/education-seminary-may-lose-accreditation.html.

[93] Samuel Weiss, 06/19/1991, "Accrediting Agency and Seminary Agree on an Advisory Role for Women," *NY Times*, https://www.nytimes.com/1991/06/19/education/accrediting-agency-and-seminary-agree-on-an-advisory-role-for-women.html.

R-E-S-P-E-C-T

In the same way that the biblical counseling movement usurped the status quo for its certification, rejecting state approval, Bible colleges and seminaries ought to do the same when it comes to the issue of accreditation. To jettison accreditation is, admittedly, to destroy an institution's credibility in the sight of the secular world.[94] But, our loyalties were never with this world. Not only would renouncing recognized accreditation vastly reduce the costs of operation for most schools, but it would also emphasize evaluation upon different criteria: The education itself. Shouldn't our desire be for local churches to validate an institution?

There are signs within conservative Protestantism that the stigma associated with an education from an unaccredited seminary or Bible college is fading, especially among Reformed evangelicals. This is due in part to a number of highly regarded teachers and authors who have emerged with training from unaccredited institutions. For example, the late R. C. Sproul, while possessing a variety of degrees from accredited schools, also possessed a Ph.D. from Whitefield Theological Seminary. The late George Scipione, one of the founding fathers of the biblical counseling movement, also

---

[94] In the eyes of many in academia, this has already been achieved— accreditation or not. Cf. the comments of Conn who claimed that any school that affirms a confessional position at the institutional level ought to be denied accreditation on that basis. Peter Conn, 06/30/2014, "The Great Accreditation Farce," *The Chronicle of Higher Education*, https://www.chronicle.com/article/The-Great-Accreditation-Farce/147425.

possessed a Ph.D. from Whitefield. Reformed Baptist theologian James R. White possesses several degrees from conventionally accredited institutions, as well as several advanced degrees from Columbia Evangelical Seminary. Elyse Fitzpatrick, known for her work within the biblical counseling movement, has an M.A. in biblical counseling from Trinity Theological Seminary. Mark Shaw, an authority on addiction and biblical counseling, possesses a D.Min. from Birmingham Theological Seminary. Aside from the institutions mentioned above, there are a variety of other credible and faithful unaccredited seminaries that have already been well established. These include Reformation Bible College, Covenant Baptist Theological Seminary, Greenville Presbyterian Theological Seminary, Forge Theological Seminary,[95] Master's International School of Divinity, Reformed Baptist Seminary, Reformation International Theological Seminary, and The North American Reformed Seminary.[96]

Both Greenville Presbyterian Theological Seminary, Covenant Baptist Theological Seminary, and Birmingham Theological Seminary claim accreditation from an 'unrecognized accreditor,' namely, the Association of Reformed Theological Seminaries (ARTS). While there are many unrecognized accreditors and accreditation mills which have engaged in some

---

[95] The author has an earned doctoral degree issued from Forge Theological Seminary.

[96] Two of the listed institutions, namely, the North American Reformed Seminary and Forge Theological Seminary do not charge for tuition.

obvious spurious practices,[97] ARTS is not an accreditation mill. ARTS is a genuine and thought through effort at a distinctly Christian non-governmental accreditation.

Some have argued that all unrecognized accreditors are necessarily illegitimate, or even "worthless," as in the case of Rick Walston.[98] Walston has argued that if accreditation isn't recognized, it isn't real. Such a view gives away the store—subjugating theological institutions to the approval of the state by implication. If through recognized accreditation, the government is the only entity that can genuinely vouch for the credibility and legitimacy of an institution, then the government serves as the gatekeeper of higher education.[99] Walston's view is the statist view: unaccredited seminaries and Bible colleges must be satisfied with no external validation of their education and any attempt to form a Christian accreditor which de-legitimizes the role of the state is immoral. By contrast, if we recognize the division of labor between state and church, there exists no good reason to trust the

---

[97] E.g., the Accrediting Commission International (ACI), which is the recapitulation of the now defunct International Accrediting Commission, which was shut down for fraud by the Attorney General of Missouri in 1989. See Walson, 87. ACI "accredits" Bible colleges and seminaries even if they teach cultic doctrine. For example, ACI accredits Atlanta Bible College, the undergraduate institution of a non-trinitarian restorationist cult.

[98] Walston, 66.

[99] See Blumenstyk's statement, "Accreditors are hugely powerful gatekeepers," in Hübner, "Obstacles to Change," 22.

government to validate theological education and any accreditation should come from the body of Christ. This is the logic of ACBC, the Evangelical Council for Financial Accountability, and it is the logic behind ARTS.

On the Legality of Operating an Unaccredited Seminary or Bible College

Currently, there are twenty-eight states which offer a religious exemption to higher education licensing, accreditation, and certification. In these states, unaccredited religious institutions operate with general autonomy, although some states require religious modifiers in the degrees issued by these institutions. Twenty-two states afford religious institutions no exemption,[100] effectively precluding any unaccredited Bible college or seminary from issuing degrees.[101] The rationale traditionally put forward by those states who possess no religious exemption is that the lack of such an exemption effectively outlaws degree mills. Such laws, however, are fine examples of gross unconstitutional

---

[100] This may change as Illinois' legislature is currently evaluating a deregulation bill (Senate Bill 2822). Cf. Morgan Lee, 03/26/2015, "Should Unaccredited Bible Colleges Be Allowed to Grant Degrees?," *Christianity Today*, https://www.christianitytoday.com/ct/2015/april/should-unaccredited-bible-colleges-be-allowed-grant-degrees.html.

[101] See for example, Public Act No. 13-118 in my home state of Connecticut: "No person, school, board, association or corporation shall operate a program of higher learning or an institution of higher education unless it has been licensed or accredited by the State Board of Education Office of Higher Education, nor shall it confer any degree unless it has been accredited in accordance with this section."

overreach since states cannot legally preclude religious higher education or the establishment of religious schools of higher education designed for ministerial training. The domain of Christian education for ministry belongs to the church.

It has become virtually impossible for those states who do not afford a religious exemption to enforce or uphold their prohibitions of unaccredited religious colleges and seminaries since the landmark ruling in HEB Ministries Inc. v. Texas Higher Education Coordinating Board. In 1999, the state of Texas issued a $173,00 fine to Tyndale Theological Seminary for issuing degrees apart from recognized accreditation or state certification and for identifying itself as a "seminary" apart from state consent. Arguing the unconstitutional nature of the Texas Education Code via the Free Speech Clause, Free Exercise Clause, and the Establishment Clause, the Supreme Court of the State of Texas ruled in favor of Tyndale in 2007.[102] Douglas Laycock, Distinguished Professor at the University of Virginia School of Law, concluded, "The state has no business licensing seminaries or any other religious institution. It is shocking that the state even attempted such regulation."[103]

INSURGENCY: A WAY FORWARD

Just as ACBC blazed a trail and established its

---

[102] Reeve Hamilton, 12/09/2011, "Questions Surround Unregulated Institutions," *NY Times*, https://www.nytimes.com/2011/12/09/us/questions-surround-unregulated-institutions.html.

[103] Douglas Laycock, *Religious Liberty*, Vol. 2 (Grand Rapids, MI: Eerdmans, 2011), 606.

own certification using biblical parameters, Christian colleges and universities ought to do the same. Transparency is critical to the de-stigmatization of legitimate Christian Bible colleges and seminaries that lack recognized accreditation. Unaccredited Christian schools should always reveal their faculty, method of education, and they should clearly and unapologetically reveal their syllabi from the outset. Schools should also make all theses and dissertations available to the public. Such transparency can serve as a means unto distinguishing a legitimate institution from a degree mill which either sells degrees and(or) issues them upon the basis of substandard work. Unaccredited institutions should not hide the fact that they reject recognized accreditation. Rather, schools should treat their lack of accreditation as a badge of honor. A great way to divulge an institution's commitment to biblical fidelity is to say, "We reject approval from governmental accreditors and are seeking the approval of Christ through his church." Further, reciprocity agreements between institutions that share theological vision ought to further grant prospective students a real means of evaluation.

4

ON PSYCHOLOGY & PSYCHIATRY

Michael R. Burgos

Adams' argument against psychological theory succeeds only if one presupposes the authority of the doctrine of plenary verbal inspiration.
—E. S. Only[104]

Fifty years ago Jay E. Adams, the father of the modern biblical counseling movement, concluded that psychology and its "illegitimate child" (i.e., psychiatry) are in serious trouble.[105] The basis for Adam's assertion was that despite its grandiose claims to the contrary, the

---

[104] Elizabeth S. Only, 1999, "Rescue the Perishing, Care for the Dying: An Analysis of Jay E. Adams' Argument Against the Use of Psychological Theory in Pastoral Counseling," Boston Univ. School of Theology, Th.D. Diss., 160.

[105] Jay E. Adams, *Competent to Counsel* (Grand Rapids, MI: Zondervan, 1970), 1.

interventions offered by psychology and psychiatry didn't work. Today, the conclusions Adam's drew in the 1970s have been validated *ad infinitum* by the crises in psychology and psychiatry. This chapter seeks to provide a concise articulation of a few of the problems within these disciplines, demonstrating that the evaluation issued by Adams in the 1970s has continued to find validation.

THE UNEMPIRICAL SCIENCE

In 2012, Ed Yong, a science journalist, published an article in *Nature* which outlined a few of the significant methodological problems inherent in research psychology. According to Yong, the vast majority of research results published in major psychology journals are incapable of being reproduced.[106] Yong cited Chris Chambers, Professor of Cognitive Neuroscience at Cardiff University, who noted that "High impact journals often regard psychology as a sort of parlour-trick…When we review papers, we're often making authors prove that their findings are novel or interesting."[107] Chambers continued, "We're not often making them prove that their findings are true."[108] Similarly, Scott Lilienfeld and Irwin Waldman have recognized the scandalous nature of this crisis:

---

[106] Ed Yong, 5/16/2012, "Replication Studies: Bad Copy," *Nature*, 485.7398, 299. Cf. Christopher J. Ferguson, 05/19/2015, "'Everybody Knows Psychology Is Not a Real Science,'" *American Psychologist*, 7.41, 527-42; John Horgan, 07/01/2016, "Sizing Up Psychology's Credibility Crisis," *Scientific American Mind*, 27.4, 18-19.

[107] Ibid.

[108] Ibid.

Indeed, in the pages of our field's most prestigious journals…scholars across diverse subdisciplines have maintained that the standard approaches adopted in published psychological investigations tend to yield a disconcertingly large number of false positive findings.[109]

How significant is this problem? In 2015, the Open Science Collaboration (OSC) published an assessment of the replications of one hundred studies published in three of the most prestigious psychological journals. OSC found that "A large portion of replications produced weaker evidence for the original findings despite using materials provided by the original authors, review in advance for methodological fidelity, and high statistical power to detect the original effect size."[110] Further, OSC found that *only one-third* of the replications attested to the findings of the original studies.

TRUST US, WE'RE THE EXPERTS…

Despite being repeatedly outed as about as scientific as alchemy, research psychology and its resultant therapies still find considerable support within both the church and the general public. This is partially due to psychology's continual effort to market itself as a necessary and effective means unto human flourishing.

---

[109] Scott O. Lilienfeld, Irwin D. Waldman eds., *Psychological Science Under Scrutiny: Recent Challenges and Proposed Solutions* (Hoboken, NJ: Wiley-Blackwell, 2017), xxi.

[110] Open Science Collaboration, 08/28/2015, "Estimating the reproducibility of psychological science," *Science*, 349.6251.

Articles frequently emerge touting the effectiveness of psychotherapy, reinforcing psychology's place as a bona fide science. One such article, published by the American Psychological Association (APA), claimed, "Psychotherapy is effective, helps reduce the overall need for health services and produces long-term health improvements." To substantiate its claim, the APA cited "more than 50 peer-reviewed studies."[111] That is, the same psychological establishment whose studies are legitimate only one-third of the time has also claimed upon the basis of "more than 50 peer-reviewed studies," that its therapies work. Moreover, several bombshell studies have emerged that suggest psychology's confidence is vastly misplaced. For instance, one study published in 2015 concluded that the efficacy of psychology's interventions for depression has been significantly overstated.[112] Purveyors of cognitive-behavioral therapy (CBT), the current "gold standard"[113] in psychotherapy, have been shown to

---

[111] 2012, "Research Shows Psychotherapy Is Effective But Underutilized," *American Psychological Association*, https://www.apa.org/news/press/releases/2012/08/psychothera py-effective.

[112] Ellen Driessen, Steven D. Hollon, Claudi L. H. Bockting, Pim Cuijpers, Erick H. Turner, 09/30/2015, "Does Publication Bias Inflate the Apparent Efficacy of Psychological Treatment for Major Depressive Disorder? A Systematic Review and Meta-Analysis of US National Institutes of Health-Funded Trials," *PLoS One*, 10.9, https://doi.org/10.1371/journal.pone.0137864.

[113] Daniel David, Ioana Cristea, Stefan G. Hofmann, 01/29/2018, "Why Cognitive Behavioral Therapy Is the Current Gold Standard of Psychotherapy," *Frontiers in*

massively exaggerate the effectiveness of CBT. One meta-data study indicated that *only seventeen percent* of trials of CBT for depression and anxiety were shown to be effective.[114]

One might imagine, given this sordid state of affairs, that psychology would dampen its enthusiasm for itself. Hardly. Brian Hughes, Professor of Psychology at the National University (Ireland), has observed that even though psychology "considers itself agile at producing authentic insights about the human psyche,"[115] it actually suffers from "excessive self-esteem:"[116]

> As attempts to replicate their research produce a mounting series of damp squibs, you might expect that by now psychologists will have become quite cautious. Psychologists should be nervous about the way their popular paradigms contradict each other: they should surely realize that one theoretical explanation is difficult to defend alongside another that is its exact opposite. Psychologists should be equally apprehensive about their vague and imprecise approaches to measurement. They should be

---

Psychiatry, 9.4, https://www.ncbi.nlm.nih.gov/pmc/articles/PMC5797481/.

[114] Falk Leichsenring, Christiane Steinert, 2017, "Is Cognitive Behavioral Therapy the Gold Standard for Psychotherapy? The Need for Plurality in Treatment and Research," *Journal of the American Medical Association*, 318.14, 1323-4.

[115] Brian M. Hughes, *Psychology in Crisis* (London, UK: Palgrave, 2018), 119.

[116] Ibid., 120.

obsessed with equivocation: after all, those margins of error must mean something. Their statistical struggles...should breed additional trepidation. Psychologists should surely react by limiting the ambition of their inferences. And each time they remember that their research captures just a thin snippet of the world's population, psychologists must feel the torrents of collective embarrassment running down their spines.[117]

Psychiatry similarly suffers from a self-esteem problem. Electroconvulsive therapy (ECT) or what is more popularly known as "Shock Therapy," is a well-hyped intervention designed to aid people with either severe or persistent emotional disorders.[118] In ECT, epileptic seizures are introduced to the brain while a person is under general anesthesia through the use of a device.[119] Eighty-five percent of those who undergo ECT are seeking relief from depression.[120] This, in itself, is curious since no known pathology causes depression.[121]

---

[117] Ibid., 119.

[118] Max Fink, *Electroshock: Healing Mental Illness*, (New York: Oxford Univ. Press, 1999), 1.

[119] Ibid.

[120] A. Rajendran, V. S. Grewal, Jyoti Prakash, 04/2015, "Does Criticism of Electroconvulsive Therapy undermines its benefits: A Critical Review of its Cognitive Adverse Effects," *Delphi Psychiatry Journal*, 18.1, 160.

[121] Gregor Hasler, 10/09/2010, "Pathophysiology of Depression: Do We Have Any Solid Evidence of Interest to Clinicians?," *World Psychiatry*, 9.3, 155-61.

Thus, introducing seizures into someone's brain to "cure" depression is obviously misguided.

Like the popular "chemical imbalance" theory, ECT relies upon a reductionistic view of the human person that rejects the existence of the immaterial soul. What the anxious and depressed person needs is the wisdom of God's Word, sound teaching, compassion for their suffering, and prayer—not a brain seizure (Psa. 23:4; Prov. 12:25; Matt. 11:28; 1 Pet. 5:7). Moreover, the terrible side effects of ECT are numerous and well documented.[122]

Scientifically, ECT and its supporting studies have been shown to have grave problems. In 2010, Drs. John Read and Richard Bentall conducted a meta-data study that analyzed all scholarly literature published on ECT with particular emphasis on depression. In this study, Read and Bentall noted that the *vast majority* of ECT studies neglected to include a placebo.[123] Further, Read and Bentall found several other methodological problems with almost all of the other ECT studies. After their comprehensive review of the literature, Read and Bentall concluded with another scientist who wrote, "There is no evidence at all that the treatment has any benefit for anyone lasting beyond a few days…The short-term benefit that is gained by some simply does not warrant the risks involved."[124]

---

[122] Ibid., 160-3, John Read, Richard Bentall, 2010, "The effectiveness of electroconvulsive therapy: A literature review," *Epidemiologia e Psichiatria Sociale*, 19.4, 342-4.

[123] Ibid., 334.

[124] Ibid., 344.

MARKETING ILLNESSES

We might ask, "Hasn't the world benefitted from psychology's identification of mental illnesses?" The innumerable disorders present in the *Diagnostic and Statistical Manual*, 5th Ed. (DSM-V), have been well observed to be inordinate.[125] Do you *really need* that cup of coffee in the morning? You likely have "Caffeine Use Disorder."[126] Obsessed with that new video game? You've got "Internet Gaming Disorder."[127] Or, are you nervous in situations where you might be embarrassed? According to the DSM-V, you may have "Social Anxiety Disorder." Given the DSM-V's range of "disorders," it is no wonder why one in four to five adults in the U.S. are said to have a mental illness.[128]

Psychology and psychiatry have effectively marketed the existence and even causality of certain major DSM-V disorders to the general public and this without basis or warrant. Bipolar disorder, in its various iterations, is a case in point. Bipolar is something of a

---

[125] Allen Frances, *Saving Normal: An Insider's Revolt Against Out-Of-Control Psychiatric Diagnosis DSM-5 Big Pharma and the Medicalization of Ordinary* (New York: William Morrow & Company, 2014).

[126] *Diagnostic Statistical Manual*, 5th Ed. [DSM-V] (Washington, DC: American Psychiatric Publishing, 2013), 792-3.

[127] Ibid., 795.

[128] Kathleen Ries Merikangas, Marcy Burstein et al., 2010, "Lifetime prevalence of mental disorders in U.S. adolescents: results from the National Comorbidity Survey Replication--Adolescent Supplement (NCS-A)," *Journal of the American Academy Child Adolescent Psychiatry*, 49.10, 980-9.

catchall diagnosis that is dependent upon a perceived set of symptoms.[129] There is currently no known pathological cause for bipolar, and subsequently, there is no treatment known to the medical community "that provide[s] sustained, symptomatic, and functional recovery."[130] Indeed, one scholarly assessment of bipolar has concluded, "From a neurobiological perspective there is no such thing as bipolar disorder."[131] Yet, bipolar is routinely characterized as a "brain disease" by the psychiatric and psychological communities. While the symptoms experienced by those who are said to have either bipolar I or II are entirely genuine, misidentifying these symptoms as a "brain disease" is antithetical to providing genuine help.

Psychotherapy's Moral Vacuum

Steaming from Freud's insistence that psychotherapy lands within the realm of the scientific[132] (i.e., as a clinical expression of psychological science), psychotherapy has sought to portray its practice as an objective and "value-free" discipline. However, it is undeniable that there exists a set of moral presuppositions that underly psychotherapy. One cannot give a word of counsel without presupposing what is right and wrong. One cannot quantify therapeutic effectiveness or even

---

[129] DSM-V, 121-39.

[130] Vladimir Maletic, Charles Raison, 08/25/2014, "Integrated Neurobiology of Bipolar Disorder," *Frontiers in Psychology*, 5.98, 1.

[131] Ibid.

[132] Jeremy Holmes, 1996, "Values in Psychotherapy," *American Journal of Psychotherapy*, 50.3, 259-60.

"mental health" without first rooting these concepts in a system of moral truths. The question is, therefore, from whence do these morals come? What is the moral grounding for the psychotherapist's counsel? Are the relevant moral commitments of therapists divulged to their counselees before the giving of counsel? More likely, psychotherapists merely impose their personal moral commitments upon their clients under the pretense of "science."

CBT, for example, operates upon the basis of a great variety of undefined moral concepts (e.g., "meaning," "dysfunction," "good/bad thoughts," "improved behavior"):

> In a nutshell, the cognitive model proposes that dysfunctional thinking (which influences the patient's mood and behavior) is common to all psychological disturbances. When people learn to evaluate their thinking in a more realistic and adaptive way, they experience improvement in their emotional state and in their behavior.[133]

Never are these moral concepts fleshed out in the literature and are instead merely assumed in practice by the therapist or counselee. Tellingly, some researchers in the field have proposed ethical training for therapists in

---

[133] Judith S. Beck, *Cognitive Behavioral Therapy: Basics and Beyond,* 2nd Ed. (New York: The Guilford Press, 2011), 3.

order to fill the moral vacuum.[134] Others have proposed the equivalent of a married bachelor: moral neutrality.[135]

PSYCHOLOGY'S CRISIS AND BIBLICAL COUNSELING'S INTEGRATIONIST CRITICS

In his magisterial *Foundations for Soul Care*, Christian Psychologist Eric Johnson correctly identified the Biblical Counseling Movement's (BCM) belief that "psychology itself is not really a science but a pseudo-science."[136] To this Johnson offered the following rebuttal:

> But the scientific basis of most contemporary psychology is beyond dispute in contemporary academia, because of its now voluminous, well documented and replicated studies in areas like

---

[134] E.g., in her study, Popescu has noted that, "Ethical questions and moral dilemmas are an important part of the therapeutic or philosophical counseling process that cannot be neglected…Existential issues are of utmost importance in both types of practices, since issues like meaning, scope, death, freedom and isolation are intrinsic to the human conditions…" Beatrice A. Popescu, 2015, "Moral Dilemmas and Existential Issues Encountered Both in Psychotherapy and Philosophical Counseling Practices," *Europe's Journal of Psychology*, 11.3, 520. Cf. Michelle J. Pearce, Harold G. Koenig et al., 03/2015, "Religiously Integrated Cognitive Behavioral Therapy: A New Method of Treatment for Major Depression in Patients With Chronic Medical Illness," *Psychotherapy*, 52.1, 56-66.

[135] Richard C. Springer, 1994, "Morality and the Practice of Psychotherapy," *Pastoral Psychology*, 43, 81-91.

[136] Johnson, *Foundations for Soul Care*, 112. Cf. Daryl H. Stevenson et al. eds., *Psychology & Christianity Integration* (Batavia, IL: Christian Association for Psychologist Studies, 2007), 53.

neuropsychology, cognition, motivation, emotion, social psychology, personality, as well as psychopathology and psychotherapy, a judgment confirmed by scientists in other disciplines...[137]

Johnson's claim is simply wrong. The "scientific basis of most contemporary psychology" is thoroughly in dispute due to psychology's long-standing replication crisis, a penchant for academic boondoggery, and its incessant medicalization of conventional human behaviors. Further, it is evident that scientists in other disciplines reject psychology as a science. For example, Alex Berezow, a microbiologist wrote:

> Psychology isn't science. Why can we definitively say that? Because psychology often does not meet the five basic requirements for a field to be considered scientifically rigorous: clearly defined terminology, quantifiability, highly controlled experimental conditions, reproducibility and, finally, predictability and testability.[138]

We should also note that there is often a palpable gap between psychological 'science' and what goes on in the clinical setting. Hence, even if one were to redefine

---

[137] Ibid., 112.

[138] Alex B. Berezow, 07/13/2012, "Why Psychology Isn't Science," *LA Times*, https://www.latimes.com/opinion/la-xpm-2012-jul-13-la-ol-blowback-pscyhology-science-20120713-story.html. Cf. 2009, "Psychology: a reality check," *Nature*, 461, 847.

"science" in order to grant validity to psychology, there would be little reason to extend that validity to clinical psychology:

> Some practitioners in clinical psychology and related mental health disciplines appear to making [*sic*] increased use of unsubstantiated, untested, and otherwise questionable treatment and assessment methods. Moreover, psychotherapeutic methods of unknown or doubtful validity are proliferating on an almost weekly basis.[139]

Adams and the BCM have issued criticism not merely at psychological science, but at the entire edifice of psychology, including its therapeutic applications.

CONCLUSION

In many ways, psychology and psychiatry are akin to those chained within the confines of Plato's cave: Both are disciplines that confidently assert their ability to understand and aid the public while failing to apprehend basic truths. The findings of these disciplines are often

---

[139] Scott O. Lilienfield et al. eds., *Science and Pseudoscience in Clinical Psychology* (New York: The Guilford Press, 2003), 2. E.g., the integration of Eye Movement Desenitization and Reprocessing in the clinical setting. Jennifer S. Dagia, 2017, "How Psychologists Experience and Perceive Eye Movement Desensitization and Reprocessing (EMDR)," Chestnut Hill College, Psy.D. Diss, 22-5. And Kelly who has argued for the integration of Reiki: William D. Kelly Jr., 2009, "The Effectiveness of Reiki as a Complement to Traditional Mental Health Services," Northcentral Univ., Ph.D. Diss., 41.

both contradictory and dubious, and many of the therapies purported to help hurting people are, in reality, ineffective and detrimental.

5

ON BODY-SOUL DUALISM

Michael R. Burgos

Anthropology remains one of the key differences between catholic orthodoxy and psychology. Psychology is wedded to physicalism and by and large, reductionism, whereas Christian orthodoxy has always included an affirmation of body-soul dualism. As a result, the interventions offered by those who seek to give counsel biblically greatly differ in method, content, and approach from those counseling out of the resources of a secular worldview. This difference leaves the integrationist with the intractable task of harmonizing Christian anthropology with modalities that are rooted in an anthropology vastly different than his faith.

Stanton L. Jones has made such an attempt in his *Psychology: A Student's Guide*. Jones has proposed a "generic" form of Roger Sperry's emergentism instead of either body-soul dualism or monism.[140] On this view, the mind is owed to the processes of the physical body and is yet not the physical body. That is, the physical processes of the human body yield a sum greater than their parts, namely, "mind, spirit, or soul."[141] Jones has likened emergentism to water:

> Water…has properties that are not explicable from the characteristics of the oxygen and hydrogen atoms alone that make it up, such as the unique property of water expanding as it freezes (which is so unlike other molecular compounds.[142]

In an earlier work, Jones affirmed what he and his co-author described as "bipartite" anthropology.[143] This view is distinct from traditional body-soul dualism in that it asserts that a human person *is* the unity of both body and soul.[144] An unstated implication of this view is that the dead who subsist in a soulish existence are, somehow,

---

[140] Stanton L. Jones, *Psychology: A Student's Guide* (Wheaton, IL: Crossway, 2014), 62, n. 10. Cf. William Hasker, *Emergent Self* (New York: Cornell Univ. Press, 2001), 189-90; Eric L. Johnson, *Foundations for Soul Care* (Downers Grove, IL: IVP Academic, 2007), 332.

[141] Jones, *Psychology*, 63.

[142] Ibid., 62.

[143] Stanton L. Jones, Richard E. Butman, *Modern Psychotherapies: A Comprehensive Christian Appraisal*, 2nd Ed. (Downers Grove, IL: IVP Academic, 2011), 108.

[144] Jones and Butman wrote, "As McDonald (1982) says, persons are "constituted of a unity of these two entities" (p. 78), and hence it is not true that one aspect (the soul-spirit or the body) is the real person and the other part an add-on." Ibid., 109.

not persons. Jones and Butman imply that their bipartite anthropology is espoused by Anthony Hoekema and John Cooper, but an assessment of the relevant literature by both of these scholars shows precisely the opposite. For Cooper, "Persons are not merely distinguishable from their earthly bodies, they are separable from them and can continue to exist without them."[145]   Hoekema wrote similarly: "The condition of believers during the intermediate state cannot be a state of nonexistence or of unconsciousness."[146] By implication, Hoekema locates personhood, not in the psychosomatic entity, but in the soul such that a disembodied soul is still conscious and personal.

Among evangelicals, the popularity of anthropological monism has grown in large part due to the scholarship of Nancy Murphy,[147] Joel B. Green,[148] and others.[149] These writers reject the immaterial soul and instead explain the human mind in strictly materialistic terms. The problems

---

[145] John W. Cooper, *Body, Soul, and Life Everlasting: Biblical Anthropology and the Monism-Dualism Debate* (Grand Rapids, MI: Eerdmans, 2000), 67.

[146] Anthony A. Hoekema, *Created in God's Image* (Grand Rapids, MI: Eerdmans, 1994), 220.

[147] Nancy Murphy, *Bodies and Souls, or Spirited Bodies?* (New York: Cambridge University Press).

[148] Joel B. Green, Body, *Soul, and Human Life: The Nature of Humanity in the Bible* (Grand Rapids, MI: Baker Academic, 2008).

[149] E.g., N. T. Wright, 03/18/2011, "Mind, Spirit, Soul and Body: All for One and One for All Reflections on Paul's Anthropology in his Complex Contexts," *Society of Christian Philosophers*, Lecture. It should be noted that while Wright rejects traditional body-soul dualism, he simultaneously and robustly affirms the intermediate state.

with Christian monism are immense. Monism is a repudiation of orthodox Christianity as body-soul dualism *is the orthodox Christian view*. Not only is it codified in the creeds and confessions, but the very resurrection of Christ also presupposes it.

Because of the critical importance of body-soul dualism to the biblical faith and biblical soul care, I have provided a brief biblical defense followed by a short consideration of this doctrine within the creeds and confessions.

Body-Soul Dualism in the New Testament

The post-conversion Paul declared, "I am a Pharisee, a son of Pharisees" (Acts 23:6) and he identified that he, like the Pharisees, possessed a belief in the resurrection of the dead. Luke recorded that the Sadducees "say that there is no resurrection, nor angel, nor spirit, but the Pharisees acknowledge them all" (Acts 23:8). The religious and theological context in which the apostle Paul came was second temple Pharisaic Judaism. This tradition clearly held to body-soul dualism and its eschatology was built upon dualism. Josephus, a self-professed Pharisee who lived contemporaneously with Paul, described the Pharisees saying,

They also believe that souls have an immortal vigor in them, and that under the earth there will be rewards or punishments, according as they have lived virtuously or viciously in this life; and the latter are to be detained in an everlasting prison, but that the former shall have power to revive and live again.[150]

So too, the literature of second temple Judaism attests to the widespread belief in an immaterial soul. In his study, George Nickelsburg noted the same:

> Much intertestamental Jewish theology anticipates a future resurrection either of the body or of the soul. The dead exist in an intermediate state. Yet some do not posit an intermediate state, for they speak of an immediate assumption to heaven.[151]

By way of example, 1 Enoch, a second temple text that Peter alluded to (2 Pet. 2:4) and Jude quoted (vv. 14-15), depicts a place wherein "the spirits of the souls of the dead" dwell "until the day of their judgment." This intermediate state also possesses a separation that segregates the "spirits of the righteous," who benefit from a "bright fountain of water," from "sinners" who suffer "great torment until the day of judgment. " This scenario is not unlike that mentioned by Jesus in Luke 16:19-31, a text which is largely considered to be an inconsequential parable by anthropological monists.[152]

---

[150] *Antiquities of the Jews*, 18.13.

[151] George W. E. Nickelsburg, *Resurrection, Immortality, and Eternal Life in Intertestamental Judaism and Early Christianity*, Expanded Ed., (Cambridge, UK: Harvard Univ. Press, 2006), 222.

[152] Froom, a Seventh-Day Adventist interpreter, devotes an entire chapter to this account, arguing that it is a merely a "fable" that Christ used to make his point. LeRoy

Other second temple literature attests to the strong Jewish belief in an immaterial soul and intermediate state. For example, 4 Maccabees makes a dualistic distinction between the "body and soul" (1:20) and characterizes souls as "immortal" (14:6; 18:23) The book of Jubilees describes a time when men's "bones shall rest in the earth, and their spirits shall have much joy" (23:31) The text also describes an intermediate state wherein the faithful exist in "majesty and honor" (4:23). The Wisdom of Solomon states,

> The souls of the righteous are in the hand of God where no torment shall touch them. In the eyes of the foolish they seemed to have died, and their departure was thought to be an affliction. (3:1-2)

Scholars have long identified the Essenes with the Qumran sect (i.e., of Dead Sea scrolls fame), which is itself likely a traditional derivative of Pharisaic Judaism. Josephus noted that the Essenes too hold the "immortality of souls."[153] This characterization is confirmed by Qumranic literature itself. For example, the interpretation of Genesis 1-3 in 4QInstruction and the Two Spirits tractate both require body-soul dualism.[154]

Froom, *The Conditionalist Faith of Our Fathers*, Vol. I (Washington: Review & Herald, 1966), 239.

[153] *Antiquities of the Jews*, 18.15. There is also a possible connection between John the Baptist and the Qumran sect given the evangelist's descriptions of John and the application of Isa. 40:3 (cf. Matt. 3:3; 1QS).

[154] See C. Evans, E. H. D. Zacharias eds., *Early Christian Literature and Intertextuality*, Vol. 2., (London: T & T Clark, 2009), 114-25.

In light of the above, it is evident that the second temple tradition in which Paul aligned himself affirmed a form of body-soul dualism that was directly connected to a belief in the resurrection.[155] Further evidence that Paul affirmed this view is present in his Epistle to the Philippians. Paul wrote, "For me to live is Christ, and to die is gain…My desire is to depart and be with Christ, for that is far better" (Phil. 1:21, v. 23b). The dichotomy Paul has presented is between living "in the flesh" or departing "to be with Christ." The verb translated "depart" (Grk. *analuō*) is fairly rare in the New Testament, occurring

---

[155] In his critique of Cooper, Green asserted that "We would be mistaken were we to argue that a direct or simple line can be drawn from OT texts to Second Temple Jewish interpretation." Green, *Body, Soul, and Human Life*, 194. For Green, second temple belief in an immaterial soul and the intermediate state was not derived from the Hebrew Bible but was instead a takeover from Greek thought [cf. Peter van Inwagen, 1995, "Dualism and Materialism: Athens and Jerusalem?," *Faith & Philosophy*, 12.4, 478-9.] Green, however, neglects Paul's identification with an established second-temple theological tradition—a tradition similarly affirmed by the disciples. Why else would the disciples mistake the Lord for a "ghost" (Grk. *phantasma*; Matt. 14:26)? Moreover, the OT, which is often depicted as having an opaque anthropology [e.g., Martine Oldhoff, 2018, "The Soul in the Bible: Monism in Biblical Scholarship? Analysing Biblical Studies from a Systematic Point of View," *European Journal of Theology*, 27.2, 147-61.], clearly depicts an affirmation of body-soul dualism. For example, the *rephaim*, variously translated "shades" (ESV), "spirits of the dead" (NASB), or "spirits of the departed" (NIV), are the conscious souls of the dead who are "guests in sheol" (Prov. 9:18) and who "tremble before God" (Job 26:25). The Lord decreed that Babylon would be "greeted" by the shades (Isa. 14:9; cf. 24:14, v. 19) in judgment.

only twice. The other occurrence is Luke 12:36 and there it refers to someone "coming home" after a wedding. The term is obviously a metaphor for death, but it implies that someone is leaving to go somewhere else. In Paul's case, he was referring to a soulish existence in the presence of Christ. The resurrection is not mentioned in this passage, and therefore Paul believed that when a Christian dies, he goes on to be with Christ. If the anthropological monism or emergentism were true, in what sense could one live apart from flesh? The clear implication is that death, or euphemistically "departure," will result in the believer's immediate existence in the presence of Christ.

A similar affirmation of body-soul dualism is assumed by Paul in his discourse on the law and sin in Rom. 7:7-25. There Paul outlines how he was "killed" (Grk. *apekteinen*) when his sin was viewed in light of God's law. This law, Paul says, although it brought "death" to him, was both "spiritual" and holy, and is the appropriate imperative for Christian living. However, even though Paul is a Christian and an apostle, he admitted that he did not obey the law. He wrote,

> For I do not understand my own actions. For I do not what I want, but I do the very thing I hate. Now if I do what I do not want, I agree with the law that it is good. So now it is no longer I who do it, but sin that dwells within me. (Romans 7:15-17)

Paul then, assuming a distinction between his body and his soul wrote,

> So now it is no longer I who do it, but sin dwelling in

me. For I know that nothing good dwells in me, that is, in my flesh. For I have the desire to do what is right, but not the ability to carry it out. (Romans 7:18)

Thereafter, Paul concluded,

> So I find it to be a law that when I want to do right, evil lies close at hand. For I delight in the law of God, in my inner being, but I see in my members another law waging war against the law of my mind and making me captive to the law of sin that dwells in my members. Wretched man that I am, who will deliver me from this body of death. (Romans 7:21-24)

For Paul, his "inner being," a being which Paul elsewhere said is "being renewed day by day," is distinct from his "body," namely that "outer self" which is "wasting away" (2 Cor. 4:16; cf. Eph. 3:16). Paul's "inner being," a being which Peter calls "the hidden person of the heart" (1 Pet. 3:4), and which the psalmist calls "the inward being" (Psa. 51:6), delights in God's law, while his "body" sins and persists in rebellion. If the monist understanding were the apostle's view, the above statements would be completely incoherent.

Jesus' teaching communicates a certain affirmation of body-soul dualism. Jesus told the penitent thief, "Truly, I say to you, today you will be with me in paradise" (Luke 23:43). Froom argued that the thief died the following day and, therefore, Jesus really wasn't in paradise that day with the thief.[156] This claim betrays a clear statement of Scripture. Froom further claimed that the verse ought to be punctuated like that of the *New World Translation* (i.e., "Truly I tell you today, you will be with me in Paradise."). This rendering places the term "today" (Grk. *semeron*) prior to the comma, suggesting that Jesus was merely saying to the thief that day he would at some point be in paradise. This is an impossible rendering given that Jesus used the phrase "Truly, I say to you" over seventy times. Every other time Jesus uses that phrase or a variation thereof, the following term *always* belongs to the next clause. So too, the addition of the word "today" to the phrase "Truly, I say to you" would be superfluous.

Green has argued that "paradise" (Grk. *paradeisos*) refers not to the intermediate state but the final state (the "paradise of God," Rev. 2:7).[157] On this reading, *semeron* refers to the immediacy of the thief's experience of heaven. That is, from the thief's perspective, he would not experience the time between his death and the resurrection and subsequently, it would seem as though no time had passed between these two events. Taking *semeron* literally, Green complained, "Presumes that time experienced by the dead and by those still living is identical."[158] While that is true, there is no positive evidence that the time experienced by the dead isn't identical to the living. Rather, the natural reading of Luke

---

[156] Froom, *The Conditionalist Faith of Our Fathers*, Vol. I, 275.

[157] Green, *Body, Soul, and Human Life*, 199.

[158] Ibid., 200.

23:43 indicates that the thief was with his Lord that very day. Similarly, the souls of the martyrs cried out in Revelation 6:10, "Sovereign Lord…how long before you will judge…the earth," implying that the dead experience time much the same as the living.

Jesus' refutation of the Sadducees is perhaps his strongest statement in support of the immaterial soul and intermediate state. In Matthew 22:23-33, the Sadducees brought a question to Jesus intending to substantiate their denial of the resurrection. Their question proposed an outlandish scenario wherein a woman had managed to marry seven brothers in keeping with the Mosaic law as depicted in Deuteronomy 25:5. Each of the seven brothers had died while married to the woman, and in the view of the Sadducees, this scenario amounted to an insurmountable problem for the doctrine of the resurrection. After all, "whose wife will she be" in the resurrected state?

> For in the resurrection they neither marry nor are given in marriage, but are like angels in heaven. And as for the resurrection of the dead, have you not read what was said to you by God: "I am the God of Abraham, and the God of Isaac, and the God of Jacob"? He is not God of the dead, but of the living. (Matthew 22:30-32)

Jesus' approach was presuppositional: In appealing to Exodus 3:6, Jesus demonstrated that the patriarchs were currently alive apart from their physical bodies, and, therefore, would ultimately be resurrected. The additional clause provided in Luke's account of this narrative serves to further emphasize this point: "Now he is not God of the dead, but of the living, for all live to him" (Luke 20:38). The present active verb translated "live" (Grk. *zōsin*), requires that the patriarchs were alive apart from their physical bodies. That Moses and Elijah were familiar with Jesus and conscious apart from their physical bodies in the transfiguration account (Matt. 17:3-4) confirms this point. Thus, Jesus' response to the Sadducean dilemma demonstrates both the immaterial soul, the intermediate state, and the resurrection.

EXCURSUS ON MONIST CHRISTOLOGY

The incarnate Son of God possessed both true deity and authentic humanity simultaneously and without confusion. Orthodoxy has held that during the three days that Christ lay in the tomb, the hypostatic union remained unbroken such that Christ was a conscious human soul in the presence of the Father. Upon resurrection, Christ's soul was reunited with his physical body and he strolled out of the tomb, defeating death and effectively undoing the curse of sin.

On the monist view, Christ did not possess an immaterial soul and, therefore, monists must either say that Jesus experienced the cessation of human consciousness in the grave, but was at the same time conscious as God, or, the monist must say that Jesus, as both God and man, was dead in the grave. The first option is a form of docetism which requires that Christ is not one indivisible theanthropic person. The second option requires divine mutability and tritheism.

Jesus claimed responsibility for his own resurrection: "Destroy this temple, and in three days I will raise it up"

(John 2:19). The monist must either interpret this claim to mean the exact opposite (i.e., 'I will not raise it up') or he must affirm a docetist Christ who apart from his humanity, raised his humanity to life.

CREEDAL EVIDENCE FOR BODY-SOUL DUALISM

The Apostles' Creed is the most widely used and venerable summarization of the Christian faith. Known to the primitive church as the *regula fidei*, the Apostles' Creed has existed in one form or another for nearly eighteen hundred years and stands as the most recognizable Christian symbol outside of the cross.

The phrase "he descended to hell" is the most controversial of the creed. However, this is likely due to poor translation. Of this clause, there are three main interpretations. To some, the phrase "descended into hell" is a metaphorical reference to the sufferings of Christ upon the cross. That is, Jesus descended into hell in the sense that he bore the equivalent of hell— the full wrath and judgment of God. However, this interpretation would introduce a redundancy into the creed, as the creed already mentioned his sufferings under Pilate and his crucifixion and death. Others understand this phrase to mean that Jesus descended into actual hell (i.e., *Gehenna,* the place of damnation). Though, there is no biblical evidence either that Jesus went to hell, or that hell even exists before the day of judgment.

A better interpretation recognizes that the translation "hell" is less than ideal. The underlying Greek has *hades,* which refers not to hell but to the intermediate realm of the dead as in the story of Lazarus and the rich man. Luke

16-19-31 describes both Lazarus and the rich man as inhabiting different sections of *hades* (v. 23). While *hades* can refer to hell (e.g., Matt 16:18), it more commonly refers to the intermediate state. Indeed, "death and hades" are thrown into hell in Revelation 20:14.

The progression of the creed implies that *hades* consist of the intermediate state between Christ's burial and resurrection:

> …born of the Virgin Mary,
> suffered under Pontius Pilate,
> was crucified, died, and was buried;
> he descended to *hades*.
> On the third day, he rose again.

The creed has likely drawn upon Peter's Christological application of Psalm 16:10 at Acts 2:27: "For you will not abandon my soul to *hades*, or let your Holy One see corruption." The natural reading of 1 Peter 3:18-19 (cf. 4:6) indicates that Christ, as a conscious and disembodied soul, preached to the "spirits in prison" (i.e., those who died in the deluge). Given Peter's claims, after Jesus died, he went not only to the section of *hades* that is paradise (Luke 23:43), but he also proclaimed his victory to those in the section of *hades* reserved for the disobedient.[159]

Martin Luther, the great magisterial reformer, called the Athanasian Creed, "The most important and glorious

---

[159] The Westminster Larger Catechism agrees. It states, "Christ's humiliation after his death consisted in his being buried, and continuing in the state of the dead, and under the power of death till the third day; which hath been otherwise expressed in these words, 'He descended into hell.'"

composition since the days of the apostles." The creed stands as the definitive trinitarian symbol of the church[160] and it is this creed that identifies a Christological analog in Christian dualism: "For as the reasonable soul and flesh is one man: so God and Man is one Christ."[161] Just as a human being possesses a physical body and immaterial soul and is yet one person, so Christ, who possesses both genuine humanity and true deity, is one person.

The Westminster Confession of Faith along with its sibling, the London Baptist Confession of Faith (1689) states clearly that God "created man, male and female, with reasonable and immortal souls."[162] Much the same may be found in the Thirty-Nine Articles, the Lutheran confessions, and the symbols of Rome and the Eastern churches. In short, virtually every single historic expression of Christianity has affirmed body-soul dualism.

---

[160] Hodge wrote, "Although not issued with the authority of any council, it was soon universally admitted in the West, and subsequently in the East, and was everywhere regarded as an ecumenical symbol." Charles Hodge, *Systematic theology*, Vol. 1 (Peabody, MA: Hendrickson, 1999), 459.

[161] Cf. Epitome of the Formula of Concord, §8.9.

[162] §4.2.

6

Counseling from the Old Testament

Chris Chumita

God has given His people a tremendous gift by revealing his Word to us in both the Old and New Testaments. Christians can and should use this gift to care for the souls of men through biblical counseling. Many biblical counselors primarily use the New Testament and often neglect the Old Testament. When they do use the Old Testament, it is often used out of context or in a way that glorifies man instead of Christ. The neglect and misuse of the Old Testament stands in contrast to the biblical counseling movement's claim that all Scripture is sufficient for counseling.

The neglect and misuse of the Old Testament severely limits a biblical counselor's ability to provide biblical counsel, and as a result, the whole counsel of God is not offered. Prior to addressing the use of the Old

Testament in counseling, we must first discuss some important preliminary issues. We will briefly examine what biblical counseling is, provide a defense for the use of the Old Testament in counseling, its foundational nature, the reasons for its neglect, and how it is commonly misused.

WHAT IS BIBLICAL COUNSELING?

Biblical counseling is distinct from other counseling methodologies since it unapologetically upholds the Word of God as sufficient for counseling and it rejects methodologies derived from secular psychology. Biblical counseling also recognizes that in order to be biblical, the counsel must be Christ-centered, under the authority of the local church, and utterly dependent on the Holy Spirit.

Biblical counseling also recognizes that the Word of God is one of the ordinary means of grace that God uses not only to save his people but to transform them into the likeness of his Son, Jesus Christ. According to J. Ryan Davidson, the ordinary means of grace are "the instruments Christ ordinarily uses to birth and strengthen the faith of the elect as he is present among them."[163]

The ministry of the Word of God is done publicly through preaching and privately through counseling. In other words, biblical counseling occurs when a Christian uses the Word of God expositionally and evangelistically to help another person deal with sin, and the trials of this

---

[163] J. Ryan Davidson, *Green Pastures: A Primer on the Ordinary Means of* Grace (Palmdale, CA: Reformed Baptist Academic Press, 2019), 20.

life in a biblical way. Mark Mann points out that:

> "Exposition, application, and exhortation are the primary means for ministering the Word of God in both the Old and New Testaments. Regardless of the number of people present, God's Word is to be declared and implemented into the lives of His people both publicly and privately."[164]

IS IT APPROPRIATE TO USE THE OLD TESTAMENT IN COUNSELING?

Some counselors have questioned the appropriateness of using the Old Testament in counseling since Christians are under the New Covenant. The question itself reveals a lack of understanding of essential hermeneutical principles such as the Analogy of Scripture. This hesitation to make use of the Old Testament also discloses poor exegesis of biblical counseling's foundational text, 2 Timothy 3:16-17: "All Scripture is breathed out by God and profitable for teaching, for reproof, for correction, and for training in righteousness, that the man of God may be complete, equipped for every good work."

The apostle Paul, under the inspiration of the Holy Spirit, was predominately referring to the Old Testament when he wrote those words to Timothy since the entire New Testament canon had not yet been written. The Old Testament Scriptures were sufficient for Timothy to minister to the people of God back then, and they are fully applicable to the people of God today.

---

[164] Mark Mann, *One Ministry of the Word* (Stanley, NC: Timeless Texts, 2004), 10.

However, we now have the entire revelation of God in the New Testament which gives us a fuller understanding of the Old Testament texts. The fact that we now have a fuller understanding of the Old Testament does not diminish the need to use the Old Testament in counseling in any way. On the contrary, it strengthens the argument on why it should be used.

Since at its core biblical counseling is about pointing people to Christ, biblical counselors can use the Old Testament to point a struggling Christian to Christ. Ian Duguid reminds us that, "Centrally, the Old Testament is a book about Christ, and more specifically, about his sufferings and glories that will follow – that is, it is a book about the promise of the coming Messiah through whose sufferings God will establish his glorious, eternal kingdom."[165]

THE OLD TESTAMENT IS FOUNDATIONAL TO THE COUNSELING PROCESS

A biblical counselor must have a solid understanding of the Old Testament in order to provide biblical counsel. Foundational theological concepts that are essential to counseling are introduced or explained in the Old Testament. Below, I have summarized a few of the concepts and their import to the counseling task.

The Old Testament is foundational to the understanding of what man is and his relationship to God. It has been said that "if you get your anthropology wrong;

---

[165] Iain Duguid "Old Testament Hermeutics," *Seeing Christ in All of Scripture*, ed. Peter Lillback (Philadelphia, PA: Westminister Seminary Press, 2016), 17.

you will get your counseling wrong."[166] The book of Genesis teaches us that man was created by God and we were made in his image. Genesis establishes the fact that man is subservient and inferior to God since man's very existence is dependent on God. Also, the fact that man is made in the image of God separates man from animals. Therefore, any secular counseling methodologies that have an evolutionary presupposition must be rejected and should not be integrated into biblical counseling.

The Old Testament is foundational to understanding sin and how it entered the world. Since sin entered the world through Adam's transgression in Genesis 3, the entire world and everything in it is affected by sin. Therefore, in some way every problem that a counselee faces are the result of sin or the result of living in a fallen world. The counselee's problem may be due to his sin, or he may be the victim of someone else's sin. Other sources of suffering such as disease and death are the result of living in a fallen world.

The Old Testament is foundational to understanding the person and work of Jesus Christ. Without the Old Testament, a biblical counselor would have a truncated view of Jesus Christ and would not be able to fully grasp what the New Testament teaches about Him. Sidney Greidanus correctly points out that, "For Jesus not only taught that the Old Testament witnessed to him, but in his life he also lived out of, fulfilled, and

---

[166] This comment was made by Pastor Joe Propri in numerous biblical counseling training courses.

taught the Scriptures."[167]

The Old Testament is foundational to understanding the New Testament. Without the Old Testament, many important concepts and terms would not be able to be fully understood. Griedanus rightly noted that:

> The New Testament is filled with many other images and concepts whose meanings we cannot know without the Old Testament. Think, for example, of such concepts as God, the Kingdom of God, salvation, prophet, priest, king, atonement, law, faith, hope, love, Christ, Son of Man, good shepherd, and servant of God."[168]

WHY IS THE OLD TESTAMENT NEGLECTED IN COUNSELING?

If the Old Testament is so foundational to counseling, why is it so neglected? While there are multiple factors that lead to its neglect, the most common reasons are that many biblical counselors are unfamiliar with it, and the amount of Scripture that would need to be used in counseling.

Sadly, many biblical counselors neglect using the Old Testament in counseling due to their unfamiliarity with it. Many biblical counselors do not have a working knowledge of the Old Testament outside of the Psalms, Proverbs, the creation account, and the popular Sunday school stories. The other books of the Old Testament are

---

[167] Sidney Greidanus, *Preaching Christ from the Old Testament: A Contemporary Hermeneutical Method* (Grand Rapids, MI: Wm. B. Eerdmans Publishing Company, 1999), 32.

[168] Ibid., 29.

not regularly read or studied. Those factors, as well as being unfamiliar with the ancient culture and customs in the Old Testament, can lead biblical counselors to neglect its use.

Biblical counselors are often trained that it is best to use one verse or a small number of verses in a counseling session in order to help a counselee comprehend what is taught and how to apply it. This method often works well when counseling from the New Testament. However, when counseling from the Old Testament, large sections of Scripture often must be used in order to teach and apply its lessons in the proper context. While there are some exceptions (e.g., the many pithy statements of Proverbs) the need to look at large passages of Scripture in a counseling session goes against what many counselors are taught and often leads to the neglect of the Old Testament.

Improper Use of the Old Testament for Counseling

As previously discussed, the Old Testament is often neglected in counseling and when it is used, it is often used improperly. While there are many ways the Old Testament is improperly used in counseling, we will only discuss three of them below.

First, biblical counselors sometimes use Old Testament characters as examples of people that a Christian should or should not imitate. In other words, they use a "heroes and villains" approach to interpreting the biographical sections of Scripture. This reduces the stories to being man-centered, moralistic, and a Christless mess. According to David Murray, "This approach changes the focus of God's Word from God to man. It tends to put man and his needs in the foreground with God and his glory in the background."[169] However, this does not mean that a counselor cannot use a biblical character as an example of someone who responded to his circumstance in either a biblical or unbiblical way. The problem is when you stop there.

For example, the account of Joseph fleeing from Potiphar's wife in Genesis 39 can be used as an example of a biblical response to sexual temptation. It can also be used to bring home the truth of 1 Corinthians 10:13 that the temptation or situation that a counselee is facing, such as a false accusation, is common to man. However, the counselor should not stop there. The biblical counselor must point to the role of the Holy Spirit in resisting temptation and how the account ultimately points to Jesus. If Jesus is left out of the counsel; it is not biblical counsel.

Second, biblical counselors sometimes take Old Testament verses out of context when they apply them in a counseling room. Two verses that are often used out of context are Jeremiah 29:11 and Genesis 17:16.

The prophet Jeremiah wrote, "For I know the plans I have for you, declares the Lord, plans for welfare and not for evil, to give you a future and a hope." (Jer. 29:11). This verse has been used as a general promise by God that he would bless his children with only good things and prosperity, or make things work out the way they want them to. However, such an interpretation

---

[169] David Murray, *Jesus On Every Page* (Nashville, TN: Thomas Nelson, 2013), 55.

neglects the verse's context. Jeremiah was writing to the Jewish people before and during the time of Babylonian exile. In Jeremiah 29:11, God was promising that he will return his people to the land after a period of time and continue to provide some blessings to them in exile.

Another verse that is often taken out of context is Genesis 17:16 where God promised Abraham that he would give him a son through Sarah. This verse is sometimes used to give hope to a couple who is struggling with infertility to promise them that God will give them a child. Using Genesis 17:16 in this way is not only cruel but it also totally ignores the unique nature of God's promise to Abraham and its role in redemptive history. The promise was made to Abraham, not an infertile couple. God promised to give Abraham a child, not them.

Biblical counselors must remember that some of God's promises in the Old Testament apply to all of God's people, but some of them are only meant for the specific person or persons that they were made to. Taking a promise that was not meant to be a universal promise and applying it to a counselee's problem can create false hope and cause them to doubt God's faithfulness.

Third, the Proverbs are sometimes used in a way that reduces each proverb to a little moralistic 'nugget.' If a proverb is not exegeted properly, it can be reduced to simply good advice and warnings about the consequences of immoral behavior that can be embraced by an unbeliever.

Proverbs is perhaps the most used Old Testament Book in biblical counseling. It is a helpful text because it takes Godly wisdom and invites the reader to incorporate it into his life. Unfortunately, some biblical counselors neglect to ground the teachings into the life and work of the wise Son of Proverbs, Jesus Christ. According to Jay Adams, "Jesus Christ is the Wisdom of God. He it is, therefore, into whose likeness one grows as he appropriates and incorporates Proverbs' teaching into daily living. As a result, it is a thoroughly Christian, Christ-honoring book."[170]

PROPER USE OF THE OLD TESTAMENT FOR COUNSELING

A discussion on the proper use of the Old Testament in biblical counseling deserves a book-length treatment. However, we will briefly explore seven examples of counseling from the Old Testament, namely, Genesis 1, Exodus 20:1-17/Deuteronomy 5:6-21, the Judges, Isaiah 59:16-19, Ezekiel 36:25-27, Psalm 88, Job 1, and Ecclesiastes.

COUNSELING FROM GENESIS 1

One of the biggest problems with many gospel proclamations in the modern American church is that they do not start with God and how he is the creator of all things. Since biblical counselors often start the counseling process with a gospel proclamation, it is imperative that they help a counselee see the greatness of God and how his very existence is dependent on God.

Genesis 1 is the perfect place to go to help a counselee understand how God created everything in six literal twenty-four-hour days and to help establish his

---

[170] Jay Adams, *The Christian Counselor's Commentary: Proverbs* (Stanley, NC: Timeless Texts, 1997), 2.

excellence and Lordship. This is especially important today because many counselees have an unbiblical view of creation, man, and sin due to various evolutionary views and other unbiblical views of creation.

COUNSELING FROM EXODUS 20:1-17/DEUTERONOMY 5:6-21

The Christian is no longer under the law of God for justification, but he is still under it as a rule of life. The law of God is best summarized in the Ten Commandments (Exod. 20:1-17; Deut. 5:6-21).

During the first session or two, it can be very beneficial for a biblical counselor to help a counselee walk through the Ten Commandments verse by verse, in either Exodus or Deuteronomy, to see which commandments he is breaking by the life-dominating sin he is dealing with. Often, he will find that he is breaking many of them; walking through each of the commandments will help him have a better understanding of the magnitude of his sin. At that point, the biblical counselor can explain how Jesus Christ kept the law perfectly and how he died to make atonement for the sins of his people.

COUNSELING FROM JUDGES

Judges contains several cycles where God's people turned to idols and rejected God, suffered consequences, cried out to God for a deliverer, and are delivered. The biblical counselor ought to use the Judges to show the counselee the danger of doing what is right in his own eyes, and his need for a deliverer. However, unlike the imperfect deliverers in Judges, we have the perfect deliverer—Jesus Christ.

COUNSELING FROM ISAIAH 59:16-19

Counseling a person who is the victim of abuse or has suffered greatly at the hands of someone else can be challenging. Thankfully, God provides numerous Scriptures that can help provide a great deal of comfort to the victim. Isaiah 59:16-19 is a fine example:

> He saw that there was no man,
> and wondered that there was no one to intercede;
> then his own arm brought him salvation,
> and his righteousness upheld him.
> He put on righteousness as a breastplate,
> and a helmet of salvation on his head;
> he put on garments of vengeance for clothing,
> and wrapped himself in zeal as a cloak.
> According to their deeds, so will he repay,
> wrath to his adversaries, repayment to his enemies;
> to the coastlands, he will render repayment.
> So they shall fear the name of the Lord from the west,
> and his glory from the rising of the sun;
> for he will come like a rushing stream,
> which the wind of the Lord drives.

In these verses, Isaiah has reminded the people of Israel that the Lord sees the injustices that his people are experiencing, and he will judge the enemies of God. How do these verses apply to a counselee that has been abused or suffered injustice? Jonathan Holmes has observed:

> For the counselee who has been abused, suffered unjustly, who has been beaten down, and taken advantage of, Scripture reminds us that we serve

a God who is going to make all things right. There is no injustice or unrighteous deed which will go unaccounted for. his judgment and repayment are sure and final.[171]

COUNSELING FROM EZEKIEL 36:25-27

Helping a counselee to have a proper understanding of concepts such as the forgiveness of sin, regeneration, and the indwelling of the Holy Spirit is vital to having victory over life-dominating sin. One of the most important verses in the entire Bible that deals with those concepts is found in Ezekiel 36:25-27. It states:

> I will sprinkle clean water on you, and you shall be clean from all your uncleannesses, and from all your idols I will cleanse you. And I will give you a new heart, and a new spirit I will put within you. And I will remove the heart of stone from your flesh and give you a heart of flesh. And I will put my Spirit within you, and cause you to walk in my statutes and be careful to obey my rules.

Walking a counselee through these three powerful verses will cover the forgiveness of sins (v. 25), regeneration (v. 26), and the indwelling of the Holy Spirit (v. 27). Each of the verses can be used as a launchpad to a fuller and deeper consideration of each of the concepts.

---

[171] Jonathan Holmes, "Counseling from Isaiah," *Biblical Counseling Foundation,* https://www.biblicalcounselingcoalition.org/2014/06/11/counseling-from-isaiah/.

Discussing all three concepts straight out of the Old Testament, while pointing to the person and work of Jesus Christ, will help a counselee understand that he is a new creation in Christ and is no longer a slave to sin.

COUNSELING FROM PSALM 88 [172]

Biblical counselors often counsel Christians whose dark night of the soul seems to have no end. They feel like they have been abandoned by God since they have been crying out to God for so long and they have begun to doubt that he is even listening to their prayers. They are tempted to stop praying and to live in the darkness. In these cases, Psalm 88 can provide a great deal of comfort.

A biblical counselor can use Psalm 88 to help a counselee see that Christians can find themselves in a very lonely, dark, and depressing place for long periods of time. However, the psalmist continues to pray to God even during the midst of what seems to be a never-ending storm. Psalm 88 can be used to encourage a counselee to continue to pray to God even if it feels like he is not listening. After spending some time in Psalm 88, the biblical counselor can lead the counselee to our suffering Savior, Jesus Christ who in Matthew 27:45-46 also felt abandoned by God.

COUNSELING FROM JOB 1

Counselees can the devil for almost all of their

---

[172] This section has drawn upon Brad Bigney, "When You Feel Abandoned By God," *Association of Certified Biblical Counselor's National Conference* (Lecture, Memphis, TN, 2019).

problems and sin issues. As they discuss their problems, they inadvertently make the devil out to be omnipotent and sovereign over the world. In these cases, a biblical counselor can use Job 1 to help a counselee gain a biblical understanding of the devil and how he cannot do anything without permission from God.

Helping a counselee see that God is even in control of the devil, can help him take responsibility for his actions. By putting the devil in his proper place, the biblical counselor can point the counselee to Jesus Christ and his ultimate defeat of the devil.

COUNSELING FROM THE BOOK OF ECCLESIASTES

Biblical counselors are often called upon to counsel someone whose hope is in the present world instead of Jesus Christ. Often, the counselee knows that he should seek Christ first, but often finds himself chasing after fame, money, or material blessings. In such cases, Ecclesiastes can provide a "stern corrective for those who seek security, pleasure, and permanence here and now."[173]

The most effective method of counseling from the Ecclesiastes is done by going through the entire book with a counselee over a period of sessions instead of exegeting specific verses or small sections of the book. Doing so will help a counselee to see how Ecclesiastes is not as pessimistic as is commonly believed. It is only pessimistic if you live life in a way that is focused on the here and now, which is full of vanity. Adams explained that the vanity discussed in Ecclesiastes "is not a vanity

---

[173] Jay Adams, *Life under the Son: Counsel from the Book of Ecclesiastes* (Stanley, NC: Timeless Texts, 1999), iv.

that describes the life of one who serves God faithfully; it is a vanity that comes from serving self by living for the pleasures of a sin-cursed world."[174]

By walking through Ecclesiastes in its entirety, a biblical counselor can help a counselee evaluate his life in light of this often-misunderstood Old Testament book and to seek God first in order to find true fulfillment. It may be a long process, but it is definitely a worthwhile investment of a biblical counselor's time.

CONCLUSION

The Old Testament is a precious gift that God has given his church. In recent times, it seems that there been a surge in popularity in preaching from the Old Testament and the importance of seeing Christ as the center of the Old Testament. Hopefully, we will see a realization that all thirty-nine books of the Old Testament have much to say about the problems of twenty-first-century Christians. Using both the Old and New Testaments to help a counselee find the biblical remedy to his problem while pointing to Christ, is God-glorifying and is the proper utilization of one of the ordinary means of grace.

---

[174] Ibid., v.

7

Toward A Thoroughgoing Biblical Critique of AA[175]

Michael R. Burgos

Like Walmart, McDonald's and the Rotary Club, Alcoholics Anonymous (AA) is one of those distinctly American institutions that is ubiquitous in most cities, even operating in the basements of many church buildings. It is revealed knowledge in American culture that anyone who struggles with alcohol addiction ought to routinely participate in local AA meetings. Because of AA's acceptance within our culture, many Christians

---

[175] A version of this chapter originally appeared in Michael R. Burgos, *Counerfeit Religion: A Biblical Analysis of Cults, Sects, and False Religious Movements* (Torrington, CT: Church Militant Pub., 2019).

have accepted the role of AA within their congregation.[176] Perhaps due to their discomfort with AA's non-Christian spirituality, others have adopted a Christian twelve-step program that is methodologically derived from AA.[177]

This chapter will provide an evaluation and critique of AA in light of Scripture, comparing its teaching and presuppositions to that of a biblical worldview. Despite its ubiquity and acceptance among many evangelicals, AA is predicated upon doctrines that are completely at odds with the Bible and contrary to the Christian gospel. It will be shown that AA is, in fact, a religion that competes with the Christian faith.

The Origin of AA

In 1928, Frank Buchman, an ordained Lutheran minister, began the Oxford Group, a moralistic cult that held that through absolute honesty, purity, unselfishness, love, and confession of sin, man can achieve peace with God, even Christ.[178] The movement, also called Moral Re-Armament, affirmed a neo-Pelagian view of human nature, believing that through confession of sin and a renewed commitment to moral living, humanity could bring about a *pax humana*.[179] Conspicuously absent from the Oxford Group's teaching was any mention of the

---

[176] For a recent example of the acceptance of AA within evangelicalism see Kent Dunnington, 05/2019, "Small Groups Anonymous," *Christianity Today*, 50-5.

[177] E.g., Celebrate Recovery, Christians in Recovery, Alcoholics Victorious.

[178] Layman With Notebook, *What is the Oxford Group?*, (Oxford, UK: Oxford Univ. Press, 1933), 8, 19.

[179] Ibid., 66.

gospel of Jesus Christ. H. A. Ironside, the great evangelical theologian and pastor of Moody Church, a contemporary of Buchman, remarked that the teaching of the Oxford Group was essentially a form of Christianity without the Savior, his cross, his atonement, and his Holy Spirit.[180]

William Wilson (1895-1971), also known as Bill W., was a drunkard[181] who had a career on Wall St. until the great depression hit on "black Tuesday," 1929.[182] Wilson gave himself over to alcohol as a way to alleviate his loss, and in 1934 he met a former drinking buddy who had reached sobriety through a conversion to the Oxford

---

[180] H. A. Ironside, "The Oxford Group Movement: Is it Scriptural?," a sermon preached at Moody Church in 1943. See also J. K. Van Baalen, *The Chaos of Cults: A Study in Present-Day Isms*, (Grand Rapids, MI: Eerdmans, 1962), 277-91.

[181] Because of the inherent problems with the modern term "alcoholic," I have restricted myself to the use of the term "drunkard," an accurate rendering of the NT terms *paroinos, oinopotēs*, and *methusos*. While these terms are always rendered "drunkard" in the *English Standard Version, paroinos* (from *para* and *oinos*—one who is 'with wine' or in the NT era a "wine addict") arguably comes the closest to the sense of "alcoholic." See Walter Bauer et al, *A Greek-English Lexicon of the New Testament and Other Early Christian Literature*, 3rd Ed. (Chicago, IL: Univ. Chicago Press, 2000), 780.

[182] *Alcoholics Anonymous: The Story of How Many Thousands of Men and Women Have Recovered from Alcoholism*, 4th Ed., (New York, NY: Alcoholics Anonymous World Services Inc., 2001), 8.

Group.[183] Although Wilson wanted sobriety, he rejected the Christian faith.[184] Bill's friend responded to his hesitancy by inviting him to invent a God of his own making. He said, "Why don't you choose your own conception of God?"[185]

While in the hospital undergoing detox, Wilson was under the care of Dr. W. D. Silkworth. Silkworth instructed Wilson that alcoholism is a disease and that this disease results in a biologically driven predilection for alcohol. Out of desperation to be free from this disease, Wilson is said to have cried out from his hospital bed, "I'll do anything! Anything at all! If there be a God, let him show himself!"[186] After having a "spiritual experience,"[187] Wilson agreed to believe in "a Power greater than himself," undergoing some form of conversion.

The basis of Wilson's relationship with his own conception of God was certain works he learned while in the Oxford Group: "a moral inventory, confession of personality defects, restitution to those harmed, helpfulness to others, and the necessity of belief in and dependence upon God." These works were later featured in AA's recovery model as Wilson became convinced that these were the essential and exclusive elements needed to

---

[183] *Pass It On: The story of Bill Wilson and how the A.A. message reached the world,* (New York, NY: Alcoholics Anonymous, 1984), 33.

[184] *Alcoholics Anonymous,* 11.

[185] Ibid., 12.

[186] *Pass It On,* 121.

[187] *Alcoholics Anonymous,* 12-13.

achieve sobriety.[188]

Dr. Robert Smith (1879-1950), also known as Dr. Bob S., was a proctologist and a severe drunkard. While participating in the Oxford Group in a last-ditch attempt to find sobriety, Smith met Wilson who introduced the good doctor to the disease model of addiction. Through his own "spiritual experience," along with Wilson's aid, Smith was able to achieve sobriety.[189]

Together, Smith and Wilson went on to aid yet another "alcoholic," and thus founded the organization as it is known today. As of 2014, AA is an international organization which consists of over 115,000 local chapters or "fellowships"[190]

AA's Method

AA only admits people into their fellowships who desire to stop drinking.[191] Once admitted, other alcoholics who have reached sobriety begin to aid the newcomer to "work the steps." He or she is typically appointed a sponsor unless they were previously invited to AA by a sponsor. The sponsor is someone who has "made some progress in the recovery program and shares that experience on a continuous, individual basis with another alcoholic who is attempting to attain or maintain sobriety

---

[188] Ibid., vi.

[189] Ibid., 180.

[190] *Alcoholics Anonymous 2014 Membership Survey*, (New York, NY: Alcoholics Anonymous World Services Inc., 2014).

[191] *Alcoholics Anonymous*, 567.

through AA"[192] The sponsor encourages and helps the newcomer to attend a variety of AA meetings, promotes AA literature and teaching to the newcomer, and disciples them in the traditions of AA.[193] Sponsors essentially look after the new recruit, assisting them on their path to sobriety.

AA's recovery movement is centered around the spiritual experience that is brought about by following the Twelve Steps of Recovery:

1. We admitted we were powerless over alcohol—that our lives had become unmanageable.

2. Came to believe that a Power greater than ourselves could restore us to sanity.

3. Made a decision to turn our will and our lives over to the care of God as we understood Him.

4. Made a searching and fearless moral inventory of ourselves.

5. Admitted to God, to ourselves, and to another human being the exact nature of our wrongs.

6. Were entirely ready to have God remove all these defects of character.

---

[192] *Questions & Answers on Sponsorship*, (New York, NY: Alcoholics Anonymous World Services Inc., 1983), 7.

[193] Ibid., 14.

7. Humbly asked Him to remove our shortcomings.

8. Made a list of all persons we had harmed, and became willing to make amends to them all.

9. Made direct amends to such people wherever possible, except when to do so would injure them or others.

10. Continued to take personal inventory and when we were wrong promptly admitted it.

11. Sought through prayer and meditation to improve our conscious contact with God as we understood Him, praying only for knowledge of His will for us and the power to carry that out.

12. Having had a spiritual awakening as the result of these steps, we tried to carry this message to alcoholics, and to practice these principles in all our affairs.[194]

A BIBLICAL EVALUATION OF AA

The tenth of AA's "Twelve Traditions" states,

No AA group or member should ever, in such a way as to implicate AA, express any opinion on outside controversial issues-particularly those of politics, alcohol reform, or sectarian religion. The Alcoholics

---

[194] *Alcoholics Anonymous*, 59-60.

Anonymous groups opposes [*sic*] no one.[195]

AA intends to portray an innocuous image while remaining neutral on controversial issues. However, such an attempt at neutrality is itself non-neutral. One cannot be lukewarm on an issue such as the Lordship of Christ. Jesus said to his disciples "Whoever is not with me is against me and whoever does not gather with me scatters" (Matt. 12:30; cf. Rev. 3:15-16). An attempt at neutrality, or even silence, is itself an opinion on "controversial issues." Therefore, because A.A. intentionally rejects the exclusivist nature of the Bible's truth claims (Acts 4:12; 1 Tim. 2:5), it rejects Christianity by implication.[196]

A. AA Promotes an Unbiblical Spirituality

Although AA claims that it "is not a religious organization,"[197] it promotes and teaches its own distinct spirituality. The practice of the twelve steps is said to produce a "spiritual experience" or "awakening," just as in some form of religious conversion. According to *Alcoholics Anonymous* (i.e., the "Big Book"), "For our group purpose there is but one ultimate authority—a loving God as He may express himself in our group conscience."[198] The pamphlet, *Members of the Clergy ask about Alcoholics Anonymous*, states,

---

[195] *Alcoholics Anonymous*, 567.

[196] See Greg L. Bahsen, *Always Ready: Directions for Defending the Faith*, (Nacogdoches, TX: Covenant Media Press, 1996), 8-12, 17.

[197] *Alcoholics Anonymous*, 10.

[198] Ibid., 565.

Most members, before turning to AA, had already admitted that they could not handle their drinking—alcohol had taken control of their lives. AA experience suggests that to get sober and stay sober, alcoholics need to accept and depend upon a spiritual entity, or force, that they perceive as greater than themselves. Some choose the AA group as their "Higher Power"; some look to God—as *they understand Him*; and others rely upon entirely different concepts.[199]

When, therefore, we speak to you of God, we mean your own conception of God. This applies, too, to other spiritual expressions which you find in this book[200]

AA's spirituality is definitionally relativistic. That is, AA's foundational "spiritual method" is idolatry. What underlies AA's nebulous notion of a "Higher Power," is the belief that all conceptions of God are equally legitimate and helpful in achieving sobriety. Thus, the underlying presupposition of AA's spirituality is theological neutrality.

Biblical Christianity rejects theological relativism in the strongest possible terms (Judg. 21:25). The non-Christian's conception of God is corrupted by sin and needs correction, not embrace. There is only one God

---

[199] *Members of the Clergy ask about Alcoholics Anonymous*, Rev. Ed., (New York, NY: The A.A. Grapevine Inc., 1992), 13.

[200] *Alcoholics Anonymous*, 47.

and he is the Triune God of the Bible (Deut. 6:4; Rom. 1:18-26; Col. 2:8): "For all the gods of the peoples are worthless idols, but the LORD made the heavens" (Psa. 96:5). The existence of biblical revelation presupposes the human need for a proper understanding of God, what God requires, and man himself. Thus, AA's theological relativism is a flat rejection of biblical revelation and the Triune God.

AA has attempted to cloak its rejection of the Triune God and biblical theology by featuring the endorsement of theological liberals such as H. E. Fosdick.[201] It promotes its spirituality as religiously neutral:

> We have no desire to convince anyone that there is only one way by which faith can be acquired. If what we have learned and felt and seen means anything at all, it means that all of us, whatever our race, creed, or color are the children of a living Creator with whom we may form a relationship upon simple and understandable terms as soon as we are willing and honest enough to try. Those having religious affiliations will find here nothing disturbing to their beliefs or ceremonies. There is no friction among us over such matters.[202]

The Scriptures teach that there is no neutrality in this life, and that there is no form of "faith" through which one may have fellowship with God outside of Christ.

---

[201] *Alcoholics Anonymous*, vii.
[202] Ibid., 28.

AA's spirituality is designed to fly under the radar of Christians as somehow compatible with the biblical faith:

> We found that God does not make too hard terms with those who seek Him. To us, the Realm of Spirit is broad, roomy, all inclusive; never exclusive or forbidding to those who earnestly seek. It is open, we believe, to all men.[203]

AA's spirituality is nothing less than an attack of the exclusivity of Jesus Christ as the Savior and Mediator. One cannot know God as Father without the salvific work of Jesus Christ (John 1:12-13). Jesus contradicted AA's inclusivist spirituality by claiming, "I am the way, and the truth, and the life. No one comes to the Father except through me" (John 14:6). AA's "broad" and "roomy" path unto God is, in reality, the wide path that leads to destruction (Matt 7:13).

B. AA Calls Disease What the Bible Calls Sin

The disease model of alcohol addiction is an intrinsic and unalterable part of the fabric of AA. For AA, "Alcoholics" are not like typical people. They are instead, "bodily and mentally different" than other people.[204] Alcoholism, says AA, becomes completely involuntary,[205] such that the only thing that may stop an alcoholic from his involuntary habit is AA's "spiritual

---

[203] *Alcoholics Anonymous*, 46.
[204] *Alcoholics Anonymous*, 30.
[205] Ibid., 15.

experience" leading to an entire "psychic change:"[206]

> At a certain point in the drinking of every alcoholic, he passes into a state where the most powerful desire to stop drinking is of absolutely no avail...have lost the power of choice in drink. Our so-called will power becomes practically nonexistent.[207]

For AA, alcoholism is a disease, and alcoholics are sick.[208] However, biblically speaking, devoting oneself to an addiction to alcohol isn't merely a disease, it is the sin of drunkenness (1 Cor. 5:11; 6:10; Eph. 5:18). Edward Welch has noted,

> Since the history of drunkenness extends back to the beginnings of recorded history, the writers of Scripture were very familiar with it, probably even more than we are today. The biblical view of drunkenness—the prototype of all addictions—is that it is always called sin, never sickness. Scripture is unwavering in this teaching and relentless in its illustrations.[209]

Because AA does not accurately identify the problem, it is unable to provide a sufficient solution. The solution for drunkenness, and for any sin, is the gospel of Jesus Christ. The means by which men become made new

---

[206] Ibid., 18.

[207] Ibid., 24.

[208] Ibid., xi, 64, 115.

[209] Edward T. Welch, *Addictions: A Banquet in the Grave*, (Philipsburg, PA: P & R Pub., 2001), 22.

is the grace of God wrought in Christ and him crucified and resurrected for the forgiveness of sins and eternal life.

When AA teaches drunkards to proclaim in its twelve steps creed, "We admitted we were powerless over alcohol,"[210] it is asserting that drunkenness is not a choice people make, but a biologically driven addiction. This assertion is a clear contradiction of the Bible's teaching, that drunkenness is a choice people make, and not merely a biological reality. When the Scripture commands, "Do not get drunk with wine, for that is debauchery," it is assuming that people have a personal choice in the matter. When Peter tells believers, "For the time that is past suffices for doing what the Gentiles want to do, living in sensuality, passions, drunkenness, orgies, drinking parties, and lawless idolatry" (1 Pet. 4:3), he assumes that his readers have a conscious choice as to whether one continues in drunkenness or not. The watching world claims it is impossible to stop drinking and it is "surprised when you do not join them in the same flood of debauchery, and they malign you" (v. 4). Nonetheless, drunkenness is a choice.

The Scriptures refute AA's claim that drunkenness is altogether different than other vices:

No temptation has overtaken you that is not common to man. God is faithful, and he will not let you be tempted beyond your ability, but with the temptation he will also provide the way of escape, that you may be able to endure it. (1 Cor. 10:13)

---

[210] *Alcoholics Anonymous*, 59.

Drunkenness is not a special classification of sin that requires a unique solution. Rather, drunkenness is "common to man," and may be resisted.

In addition to there being no biblical justification for the disease model of alcohol addiction, there are also severe medical, logical, and moral problems with the model:

1. AA's Model Revokes Both Personal Freedom and Responsibility

If addiction is brought about by a genetic disease, this presupposes a loss of personal freedom and subsequently, personal responsibility. Thus, the drunk who drives his car into a crowd of people isn't personally responsible. Rather, such a turn of affairs was brought about by an illness, just as if the drunk had a stroke while behind the wheel. The mother of the baby born with a drug addiction shouldn't be prosecuted, as her actions were merely the result of a disease. If the brain disease model were true, many actions previously deemed immoral or criminal should, when committed by a drunkard, go unpunished.

2. AA's Model Presupposes Anthropological Monism

The notion that drunkenness is brought about by genetics implies that human beings are not a body-soul unity as taught in the Christian Bible. Instead, the brain disease view assumes that human beings are only physical entities who have no immaterial soul or spirit. This view, known as physicalism or monism, is in fundamental contradiction with the Bible's description of the soulish existence experienced by the dead, whether in the presence of God or in torment (Luke 16:19-31; cf. 23:43).[211]

3. *AA's Model is Intrinsically Unscientific*

The disease model assumes a completely unscientific understanding of drunkenness. Built into the model is the notion that a drunkard is someone who has an uncontrollable compulsion to drink. This lack of control is said to be evidence by destructive behaviors and failed attempts at quitting. "But, there is no scientific way to distinguish between uncontrolled compulsion and uncontrollable compulsion."[212]

4. *The Brain Disease Model is Yet Unproven*

There is not unanimity among medical professionals and scholars on the brain disease model of addiction. For instance, a recent article in *The New England Journal of Medicine* noted that, "the concept of addiction as a disease of the brain is still being questioned."[213] Consider the following:

> Although the brain disease model of addiction is perceived by many as received knowledge, it is not supported by research or logic. In

---

[211] See pp. 70-84.

[212] William Wilbanks, 12/01/1989, "The Danger In Viewing Addicts As Victims: A Critique Of The Disease Model Of Addiction," *Criminal Justice Policy Review*, 3.16, 411.

[213] Nora D. Volkow, George F. Koob,, A. Thomas McLellan, 01/28/2016, "Neurobiologic Advances from the Brain Disease Model of Addiction," *The New England Journal of Medicine*, 10.1056, 364.

contrast, well established, quantitative choice principles predict both the possibility and the details of addiction.[214]

It surely is irresponsible to claim that 'addiction' is a brain disease based on the present state of neurological knowledge and underlying theories and techniques. It is more probable that addiction is normal human bonding to an object, in spite of the negative social and cultural evaluations it is subjected to.[215]

There are many people who recover from alcohol addiction without having had any treatment for their "disease," and no actual medical intervention for the brain disease model has ever been developed. This is due to the fact that there is no pathology associated with addiction. While brain disease model advocates argue that addiction has a molecular basis in the human brain, there exists no known biological marker whatever.[216] It is more accurate

---

[214] Gene N. Heyman, 05/2013, "Addiction and Choice: Theory and New Data," *Frontiers in Psychiatry*, 4.

[215] Peter Cohen, 03/22/2009, *The Naked Empress. Modern neuro-science and the concept of addiction*, Presentation at the 12th Platform for Drug Treatment, Mondsee, Austria. https://seekhealing.org/downloads/Dr.Peter.Cohen.research-.The.naked.empress.pdf.

[216] Rachel Hammer, Molly Dingel, Jenny Ostergren, Brad Partridge, Jennifer McCormick, and Barbara A. Koenig, 2013, "Addiction: Current Criticism of the Brain Disease Paradigm," *AJOB Neuroscience*, 4.3, 27-32.

to recognize that brain function changes gradually in response to alcohol addiction.[217]

5. *AA's Model Requires Wholesale Ascent to Modern Psychology*

There is a good indication in the literature of AA that the organization affirms a modern psychological view of "mental illness" in conjunction with the brain disease model.[218] The notion of a non-pathological mental disease is contrary to the basic teaching of Scripture. As Adams notes below, the Bible doesn't possess a category for a non-organic illness:

> The Scriptures plainly speak of both organically based problems as well as those problems that stem from sinful attitudes and behavior; but where, in all God's Word, is there so much as a trace of any third source of problems which might approximate the modern concept of 'mental illness'? Clearly, the burden of proof lies with those who loudly affirm the

---

[217] Even among scholarship that favors the brain disease model, there is a tacit admission that factors such as stress, age of drinking onset, access to alcohol, and other environmental factors are determinative. For example, one study concludes, "Alcoholism is a complex disease caused by genetic and environmental factors." Such an assertion engages in question begging. Dana Most, Laura Ferguson, R. Adron Harris, "Molecular Basis of Alcoholism" in *Handbook of Clinical Neurology*, Vol. 125, 101. Cf. Shafiqur Rahman ed., *Progress in Molecular Biology and Translational Science: The Molecular Basis of Drug Addiction*, Vol. 137, (Boston, MA: Academic Press, 2016), 42ff.

[218] *Alcoholics Anonymous*, xix, 7, 30, 133.

existence of mental illness or disease but fail to demonstrate biblically that it exists. Until such a demonstration is forthcoming, the only safe course to follow is to declare with all of Scripture that the genesis of such human problems are twofold, not threefold.[219]

AA's capitulation to psychology requires a consideration of the vast problems inherent in the modern psychological establishment. Such a consideration is provided *supra*.

AA's embrace of psychology's "mental disease" concept and the brain disease model of addiction, leave AA incapable of providing those who struggle with alcohol addiction an appropriate solution. Drunkenness is first a spiritual condition, and only by implication a physiological condition. That is, the physiological effects of drunkenness are brought about by a preexisting spiritual condition, which in the case of the drunkard, is manifested in alcohol abuse. While legitimate medical interventions may be necessary, the root issue is one of sin and not disease.

C. AA's Spiritual Method Denies the Gospel

AA's slavish devotion to the disease model of addiction renders its members in a state of helplessness such that they may never achieve freedom from the

---

[219] Jay E. Adams, *Competent to Counsel: Introduction to Nouthetic Counseling*, (Grand Rapids, MI: Zondervan, 1970), 29.

predilection to be drunk. AA has cloaked its failure to provide freedom from alcohol addiction by instituting its own anthropological dogma, namely, once someone is an alcoholic, he or she will always be an alcoholic. Hence, AA members introduce themselves saying, "Hello, my name is…and I am an alcoholic," into perpetuity. Alcoholism, says AA, is a disease for which there exists no cure.[220] So devoted is AA to the disease model, the organization equates alcohol addiction with the finality of amputation:

> We know that no real alcoholic ever recovers control... We are like men who have lost their legs; they never grow new ones.[221]

By distinction, the Christian gospel makes sinners free from bondage to sin and the Holy Spirit sanctifies his people (Rom. 6:7, vv. 18-22; 8:2). While Christians may still struggle with sin (Rom. 7:7-25; 1 John 2:1), they are not a slave to sin and are a new creation in Jesus Christ (2 Cor. 5:17). Jesus said, "So if the Son sets you free, you will be free indeed" (John 8:36). The Scriptures explicitly deny the finality of addiction:

> Or do you not know that the unrighteous will not inherit the kingdom of God? Do not be deceived: neither the sexually immoral, nor idolaters, nor adulterers, nor men who practice homosexuality, nor thieves, nor the greedy, nor drunkards, nor revilers,

---

[220] *Alcoholics Anonymous*, 85.
[221] Ibid., 28.

nor swindlers will inherit the kingdom of God. And such were some of you. But you were washed, you were sanctified, you were justified in the name of the Lord Jesus Christ and by the Spirit of our God. (1 Cor. 6:9-11)

"Drunkards," says the apostle Paul, were transformed into Christians by the power of the gospel of Jesus Christ. By using the imperfect verb *ēte*, Paul characterizes some of the Corinthian Christians as precisely what AA denies, people who *were* once addicted to alcohol, but were made free from that addiction.

The biblical answer to either a substance addiction or a behavioral addiction (i.e., one that is not in and of itself sinful) is not complete abstinence. For instance, the Bible's message to someone who is a glutton and is addicted to overeating is not, "Stop eating, and never eat again." Instead, the Bible's message is to repent from abusing the gift of food, and use food properly through the redemptive power of the gospel of Jesus Christ and his Holy Spirit. Similarly, no one says to the shopping addict, "Never buy things again." Rather, the Bible's directive is to put the gift of provision within its appropriate place. So it is with alcohol addiction. Fear of relapse such that one may never drink alcohol again is not recovery. Rather, recovery is a well-adjusted and faithful disposition that is not still in bondage to sin. The Christian who has been freed from the sin of drunkenness is free to make good use of God's gift of alcohol. Indeed, that Jesus ordained the use of alcohol in the Lord's Supper is good evidence that neither he nor his church viewed complete abstinence as the proper approach to drunkenness. The wealth of so-called "dry drunks" in AA testifies that its methods are able only to bring people to a fearful state wherein the potential relapse is always close at hand.

CONCLUSION

AA is in no way compatible with biblical Christianity, and it is in itself another a competing religion—The AA fellowships are its churches, the 'Big Book' is its Bible, the "spiritual experience" is its conversion, sponsors are its clergy, and the Twelve Steps are its creed. AA's religion even possesses a method of evangelism complete with personal testimony:

When you discover a prospect for Alcoholics Anonymous, find out all you can about him. If he does not want to stop drinking, don't waste time trying to persuade him. You may spoil a later opportunity. This advice is given for his family also. They should be patient, realizing they are dealing with a sick person.[222]

Tell him [i.e., the prospect] exactly what happened to you. Stress the spiritual feature freely. If the man be agnostic or atheist, make it emphatic that he does not have to agree with your conception of God. He can choose any conception he likes, provided it makes sense to him. The main thing is that he be willing to believe in a Power greater than himself and that he live by spiritual principles.[223]

---

[222] *Alcoholics Anonymous*, 90.
[223] Ibid., 93.

In the final analysis, AA is a competing religion, and only through religious syncretism, can one harmonize the competing claims of Christianity and AA While many have reached sobriety through AA, the end doesn't justify the means. Millenia before AA existed, those who were addicted to alcohol found healing and freedom through the gospel of Jesus Christ, Christian soul care, and the local church.

8

AN ASSESSMENT OF CREATION THERAPY

Michael R. Burgos

Within ancient Greece, Hippocrates[224] speculated that creation was comprised of four elements, namely, earth, air, fire, and water. He further conjectured that the human constitution mirrors the earth's composition such that the human body functions upon the basis of four "humors:" blood, phlegm, yellow bile, and black bile.

---

[224] There is some uncertainty as to whether these theories may be properly attributed to Hippocrates. Jouanna has noted that the theory of the four humors first occurs in the writings of Polybus, a student of Hippocrates. See Jacques Jouanna's "The Legacy of the Hippocratic Treatise the Nature of Man: The Theory of the Four Humors," in Philip Van Der Eijk ed., *In Greek Medicine from Hippocrates to Galen: Selected Papers* (Leiden, NL: Brill, 2012), 335-6.

Hippocrates attributed good health to a proper balance of the humors. Conversely, bad health or a bad state of mind was attributed to a humoral imbalance.

Hippocrates' theory would go on to dominate medicine for several millennia until the scientific age would dismiss it as a fanciful and dangerous myth.[225] However, long prior to being dispelled, Hippocrates' theory would be developed into a primitive personality theory. Galen, a second-century physician, extrapolated humoral theory and determined that there were four personality types or "temperaments:" sanguine, choleric, melancholic, and phlegmatic.

> The sanguine type was even-dispositioned, warmhearted, optimistic, and energetic. The choleric was quick to action, assertive, and prone to hostility and anger. Depression, sadness, and anxiety characterized the melancholic. The phlegmatic type was listless and lethargic.[226]

Several twentieth-century psychologists would build upon temperament theory, having long since jettisoned its humoral aspects. Today, however, most of the major schools of psychology prefer other explanations for human personality (e.g., social-cognitive and

---

[225] Hunt notes that bloodletting, a popular means unto balancing the humors, had caused "incalculable" harm.
Morton Hunt, *The Story of Psychology* (New York: Anchor Books, 2007), 18.
[226] D. G. Benner, P. C. Hill eds., *Baker Encyclopedia of Psychology and Counseling*, 2nd Ed. (Grand Rapids, MI: Baker, 1999), 1233.

psychodynamic theories).

TEMPERAMENT THEORY FINDS A PLACE IN THE CHURCH

In 1996, Tim LaHaye published *Spirit Controlled Temperament*, introducing temperament theory to a Christian audience. His book resonated with evangelicals, eventually selling over one million copies. To summarize, LaHaye's presentation asserts several key principles of contemporary temperament theory: "Temperament is the combination of traits we were born with; character is our 'civilized' temperament; personality is the 'face' we show to others."[227] According to LaHaye, it is impossible for temperaments to change, but the Holy Spirit can "modify" our temperaments such that they appear to be changed.[228] Further, "We are all a blend of at least two temperaments: One predominates; the other is secondary."[229] Lastly, LaHaye introduced the "LaHaye Temperament Analysis," such that people may discover their inborn temperament blend.

LaHaye never attempted to find biblical justification for the four temperaments except to assert: "In Proverbs 30:11-14 the wise man saw four kinds of people. About five hundred years later, the four were given names by Hippocrates."[230] What LaHaye didn't tell his readers was that a contextual reading of Proverbs 30

---

[227] Tim LaHaye, *Spirit Controlled Temperament* (Tyndale House Pub., 1994), 16.
[228] Ibid., 19.
[229] Ibid., 51.
[230] Ibid., viii.

reveals that the four kinds of people cited by the proverbist refer to four varieties of wicked people:

> There are those who curse their fathers and do not bless their mothers.
> There are those who are clean in their own eyes but are not washed of their filth.
> There are those—how lofty are their eyes, how high their eyelids lift!
> There are those whose teeth are swords, whose fangs are knives, to devour the poor from off the earth, the needy from among mankind. (Proverbs 30:11-14, ESV)

The term translated "There are those" (Heb. *dôr*) is literally translated "generation," and refers not to four temperaments, but of four varieties of people who break God's commandments. The first group violates the fifth commandment; "Honor your father and mother" (Exod. 20:12). The second group is guilty of hypocrisy, believing that they are "ritually clean" (Heb. *ṭāhôr*, cf. Deut. 23:12–14), but are instead covered in their own "excrement." The third group is guilty of arrogance and pride, and the fourth group is guilty of using speech to destroy others, especially the poor (cf. Prov. 25:18).

Despite his attempt, LaHaye's iteration of temperament theory has absolutely no biblical (or scientific) basis—not one shred. The Bible never states that our "temperament" is determined by our heredity and it never teaches us that our sin is ultimately a result of weakness brought about by our temperament.[231] The Bible doesn't even acknowledge the category of "temperament." Adams well observed:

> [LaHaye's] categories came from paganism, not from Scripture…Surely the framework for a system of counseling ought to arise from biblical exegesis, not from pagan Greek philosophy…[232]

LaHaye's theory is little more than a pseudo-scientific form of biological determinism baptized into Christianese; the resurrection of ancient pagan folk-psychology dressed in church clothes.

CREATION THERAPY

Richard Arno and his wife Phyllis are credited with designing their own Christian alternative to secular psychology. This method, entitled "Creation Therapy," is essentially a therapeutic adaptation of LaHaye's temperament theory. It includes a fifth temperament, the supine, which is alleged to refer to a conscientious and servile person.

Like LaHaye, the Arnos claim that mankind has an inborn temperament that "determines how he reacts to

---

[231] I am not suggesting that people are not born with certain tendencies, both in character and disposition. These creational differences, however, are not to be confused with immutable temperaments born of heredity.

[232] Jay E. Adams, *The Practical Encyclopedia of Christian Counseling* (Stanley, NC: Timeless Texts, 2003), 175.

people, places, and things."[233] This "inborn" and immutable temperament is cited in distinction with the belief that "people are born as blank slates," a viewpoint the Arnos claim was originated by Thomas Aquinas. This is a completely spurious claim as Aquinas held an anthropology that was thoroughly in line with Christian orthodoxy. In attributing the doctrine of *tabula rosa* to Aquinas, the Arnos have misunderstood this concept, having taken it to mean that the human mind and character are formless at birth. This, however, is a simplistic mischaracterization since Aquinas' point in the relevant literature is that man is dependent upon his senses to give content to his experience and to express his intellect.[234] Moreover, Aquinas had a conventional doctrine of original sin: "Christ alone excepted, all men descended from Adam contract original sin from him."[235]

The Arnos claim Creation Therapy is "the mechanism by which man is given the ability to find balance between body, soul, and spirit, allowing him to be the best that God created him to be."[236] The Arnos allege that their system identifies one's "temperament needs" such that those needs can be met so that "all areas of the inner man" may be in "perfect balance."[237] Character

---

[233] Richard G. Arno, Phyllis J. Arno, *Creation Therapy*, 7th Ed. (n.p., 1983), 1.

[234] Thomas Aquinas, *The Summa Theologica of St. Thomas Aquinas*, Vol. 1 (Notre Dame, IN: Christian Classics, 1948), 421-8.

[235] Ibid., 501, cf. 415: "The sin in which a man is conceived is original sin," and "original sin infects every part of the soul."

[236] Arno, *Creation Therapy*, 19.

[237] Ibid., 18.

defects and sinful predilections are recast by the Arnos as "temperament weaknesses." Indeed, the language of sin and grace is nearly absent from *Creation Therapy*. Once a counselee's "temperament blend" is identified, counsel is issued upon that basis.

Following the example of LaHaye, the Arnos developed the "Arno Profile System" (APS)[238] to help people identify their inborn temperament. The APS is essentially a coopted version of the FIRO-B test produced by humanist and psychologist, William Schutz. Schutz introduced a theory of interpersonal relations entitled "Fundamental Interpersonal Relations Orientation" or FIRO. He argued that every person has three interpersonal needs: inclusion, control, and affection,[239] and then developed a fifty-four question test (i.e., FIRO-B) in order to measure persons according to their three interpersonal needs. The Arnos adapted the FIRO-B to fit their iteration of temperament theory calling it the "Arno Profile System."

Having obtained a copy of the APS, I examined the questions to determine if this test was a legitimate means of gathering data such that meaningful and relevant counsel could be provided. What I found was a series of surface-level questions that are largely irrelevant to the problems faced by those seeking godly counsel. The test consists of fifty-four questions which may be answered with one of six choices ranging from "never" to "usually."

---

[238] Prior to the year 2000, the Arnos called their test the Temperament Analysis Profile or TAP.

[239] J.E. Roeckelein ed., *Elsevier's Dictionary of Psychological Theories* (Amsterdam, NL: Elsevier, 2006), 218.

The questions in this test are designed to divulge what a counselee thinks about himself as it pertains to his temperament (e.g., "I let other people control my actions," and "I like people to invite me to things").

The APS is alleged to disclose what "temperament blend" the counselee has as it relates to Schutz's three categories of inclusion, control, and affection. Once one's temperament analysis is conducted via the APS, a creation therapist then attempts to issue counsel upon the basis of the set of preconceived attributes that are associated with the counselee's temperament. As one National Christian Counselors Association (NCCA)[240] certified counselor put it, "Temperament holds the answers to every relationship problem."[241]

The trouble with this methodology is obvious: NCCA counselors are not counseling people, but are instead counseling temperaments. Instead of gathering data to truly understand who a counselee is and what he or she is facing, creation therapists merely find out which temperament boxes their counselee fits in so that canned responses can be offered to address the counselee's problems. Such a methodology has more in common with astrology than biblical Christianity.

At times, it is hard to distinguish the Arnos counseling methodology from immoral manipulation. For example, when counseling "the Melancholy," the Arnos

---

[240] The NCCA is a degree and licensure granting organization founded by the Arnos. See *intra*.

[241] Rick Martin, *God Created You: A Guide to Temperament Therapy* (Charlotte, MI: Jesus is Lord Ministries, 2004), 5.

insist that the counselor approach the counselee with "intellectual superiority," since people who have a melancholy temperament are "rebels."[242] They further instruct their counselors that "It is imperative that you establish your superior intelligence to this person."[243] The Arnos suggest letting melancholy counselees "see your credentials" and that "If they have a higher educational degree than you do, let them know that you have 25 years of experience."[244] Additionally, the Arnos require that their counselors "never confront a Melancholy counselee with their mistakes."[245] Not only is this approach manipulative, it is also utterly unbiblical. Jesus and his apostles taught that it is right to confront a brother with his sin in order to establish reconciliation, repentance, and righteousness (Matt. 18:15-20; 1 Tim. 5:20).

From the perspective of secular psychology, the APS/FIRO-B test fails to live up to the hype. In 2003, the Buros Center for Testing, the reputable testing organization of the University of Nebraska, evaluated the FIRO-B. The evaluation revealed significant deficiencies. The FIRO-B "appears to fall short of the mark due to flaws in conceptualization and implementation."[246]

In his text, *Case Studies: Epistlemological* [*sic*] *Validation of the Arno Profile System: Temperament*

---

[242] Arno, *Creation Therapy*, 73.

[243] Ibid., 75.

[244] Ibid.

[245] Ibid.

[246] D. Oswald, 2003, "Test review of FIRO-B(tm)," in B. S. Plake, J. C. Impara, R. A. Spies eds., *The Fifteenth Mental Measurements Yearbook*, http://marketplace.unl.edu/buros/.

Studies, Alex Appiah, a Licensed Marriage and Family Therapist, has attempted to mount a defense of temperament theory and the APS by demonstrating their efficacy via case studies. What this book demonstrates is precisely the opposite. In one case, Appiah writes of a woman named "Daniella" who sought counseling because of depression and anger. After having run her through the APS, Appiah then reviewed Daniella's "inborn" temperament traits with her. Appiah then counseled her to adjust her life to fit these traits. For example, according to the APS, Daniella is "Melancholy-Compulsive in the area of Control." Appiah then concluded that Daniella "Has a compulsive need to 'appear' competent and in control." He then counseled her to "learn to submit to authorities while maintaining control of her own personal life."[247] Not once did Appiah appeal to the gospel and its implications for this woman's life. Never was the rich treasury of biblical wisdom applied to her anger and depression. Daniella was never confronted with her sin and her need for grace. Daniella's counselor was focused upon the results of the APS and not the reality of her life.

Is the Arnos' System Biblical?

Whereas the Arnos have asserted that their theory is rooted in the Bible and is completely in harmony with the Christian faith, Creation Therapy, like that of LaHaye's temperament theory, is completely absent of biblical support. The only text Arnos have attempted to

---

[247] Alex Appiah, *Case Studies: Epistlemological* [sic] *Validation of the Arno Profile System: Temperament Studies* (n.p., 2018), Kindle Edition, loc. 1296.

marshal to demonstrate the biblical nature of their theory is, unsurprisingly, Proverbs 30:11-14. As noted above, this passage says nothing about temperaments but instead characterizes those who break the commandments of God within the context of the writer's life. So too, the Arnos have engaged in proof-texting in order to demonstrate that the human temperament is comprised of inclusion, control, and affection. They have cited a handful of texts (e.g., 1 Cor. 2:10; Luke 1:46-47; Eze. 18:31), all of which say nothing about temperament nor inclusion, control, or affection—psychological categories that are completely foreign to the biblical text.

To put it plainly, there is absolutely no biblical justification for any part of temperament theory or the Arnos' system. Whereas the Arnos make much of the fact that they reject modern psychotherapies,[248] their system is rooted in the backward thinking of an unbelieving worldview (i.e., that of Galen and those who would build on his theory), and it is thoroughly influenced by secular psychology. For example, the Arnos have appropriated the introvert/extrovert paradigm popularized by the occultist and psychologist C. G. Jung.[249] Much the same can be said regarding the Arnos appropriation of the

---

[248] Arno, *Creation Therapy*, v.

[249] While it is claimed by certain Jungian psychologists that Jung was not a "believer" in the occult [e.g., Calvin S. Hall, Vernon J. Nordby, *A Primer on Jungian Psychology* (New York: Meridian, 1999), 25.], Jung's own writings easily betray such a claim. Jung believed in the full gamut of occultism: clairvoyance, prophecy, animal magnetism, visions, divination, ghosts, human levitation, etc. See C. G. Jung, *Psychology and the Occult* (Princeton, NJ: Princeton Univ. Press, 1977).

language of "self-esteem." By implication, the Arnos' counseling methodology implies that the Bible is insufficient to equip the church for the good work of counseling (2 Tim. 3:16-17). Specifically, creation therapy presupposes that the Bible insufficiently teaches the doctrine of anthropology and counseling methodology.[250] Instead of the genuinely godly counsel given by, say, the apostle Paul, the Arnos and the NCCA, give counsel from a baptized version of an ancient and long-discredited personality theory.

The Bible does not teach that each human being has an unchanging and innate temperament. Rather, the expectation of Scripture is that Christians would change comprehensively according to the Spirit's ministry of sanctification. Instead of seeking to identify our inborn temperament to understand ourselves and our needs, the Bible directs us to live a God-focused life wherein Jesus is our greatest treasure. The Triune God calls forth, "listen to me" (Isa. 51:1), "turn to me" (Isa. 45:22). The Scripture never directs those who are afflicted to look to themselves to understand or solve their problems.

The ad-hock attributes associated with the various temperaments are completely baseless and recast human identity in a two-dimensional framework that is neither realistic nor pragmatic. Whereas the Arnos believe

---

[250] C.f., the comments made by Sewell: "The Pastor who wants to facilitate healing in the Body of Christ will seek to have a better understanding of temperament…the Word of God has to be applied in different ways according to the temperament…" Selvyn Sewell, *Pastoring the Temperament: A Guide for Pastoral Counseling* (Bloomington, IN: Xlibris, 2008), 11.

that their theory is the key to giving godly counsel, they depart from the biblical text to derive its content. Like psychology and psychiatry, temperament theory originates from the unbelieving world and is fundamentally man-centered.

The Arnos' have asserted that sin is essentially brought about as a result of unmet temperament needs.[251] Subsequently, recognizing these needs, fulfilling them, and maintaining a balance will result in individuals refraining from falling "into an area of temperament weakness." This paradigm, however, is also completely unbiblical. The command of the New Testament is not to get our "temperament needs" met, but to deny ourselves and follow Christ (Matt. 16:24). Man's sin is brought about most fundamentally by the idolatry of self and is only corrected by trust in the true God and a denial of self. Christianity then is an exercise in delayed gratification: Putting to death our selfish desires (Gal. 5:24), setting our minds "on things above, not on things that are on earth" (Col. 3:1), and patiently awaiting our glorious reward, namely, Christ himself.

> The way of the cross is for the present; glory and reward will come only in the future when Jesus comes to reign. Discipleship means certain

---

[251] Arno, *Creation Therapy*, 241. Cf. Adams' critique of the self-esteem movement which promotes a similar needs-based anthropology. Jay E. Adams, *The Biblical View of Self-Esteem, Self-Love, & Self-Image* (Eugene, OR: Harvest House Pub., 1986), esp. 41-61.

death.[252]

Unlike Creation Therapy, the Christian faith calls us to conformity to the image of Christ, and that conformity *requires* comprehensive change. Our desires, needs, character, personality, minds—indeed everything that we are must change and be conformed to Christ. Thus, whereas Creation Therapy aims to teach counselees to 'know thyself,' the Christian faith teaches counselees to set aside themselves and to know God.

Creation Therapy is predicated upon a trichotomist anthropology which asserts that mankind is a "triune being…made up of body, soul, and spirit."[253] According to the Arnos, the soul includes the human's intellect, will, and emotions (cf. Schutz), and it is "in the soul" that the Arnos have located temperament.[254] Plainly put, the Arnos' trichotomist anthropology is wrong. When God created man, he created him from two components: breath and dust (Gen. 2:7).

When we examine the manner in which the terms "soul and "spirit" are used in Scripture, it is clear that these are synonymous and refer to the same immaterial component. For instance, Mary's famous song, the *Magnificat*, states, "My soul magnifies the Lord, and my spirit rejoices in God my Savior" (Luke 1:46-47). Mary's statement is a classic example of synonymous parallelism indicating that the terms "soul" and "spirit" are

---

[252] David L. Turner, *Baker Exegetical Commentary on the New Testament: Matthew* (Grand Rapids, MI: Baker Academic, 2008), 412.

[253] Arno, *Creation Therapy*, 10.

[254] Ibid., 12.

interchangeable. John 12:27 records Jesus as saying, "Now my soul is troubled." In an entirely similar context, John 13:21 states, "Jesus was troubled in his spirit." Jesus uses soul and spirit synonymously when he says that we are body and soul (Matt. 10:28) and body and spirit (Matt. 26:41). Both the soul and spirit are characterized within Scripture as the immaterial component of man (Luke 24:29; 1 Cor. 2:11). While there are many more examples we could appeal to, suffice it to say that these terms are used synonymously. So too, the interchangeability of "soul" and "spirit" is confirmed in the lexicons. Taking these terms as they are found in the New Testament, the term *psuchē* (i.e., "soul") is defined as "life on earth in its animating aspect making bodily functions possible—life, life-principle, soul."[255] The term *pneuma* (i.e., "spirit") is defined as "that which animates or gives life to the body."[256]

Given the above, when we analyze the two principal texts marshaled in defense of trichotomy (i.e., 1 Thess. 5:23, Heb. 4:12), there exists little reason to interpret these two verses as teaching an anthropology otherwise unknown in the New Testament. When Paul wrote, "Now may the God of peace himself sanctify you completely, and may your whole spirit and soul and body be kept blameless at the coming of our Lord Jesus Christ" (1 Thess. 5:23), we ought to recognize that he "accumulates terms to express completeness, a common

---

[255] Walter Bauer et al, *A Greek-English Lexicon of the New Testament and Other Early Christian Literature*, 3rd Ed. (Chicago, IL: Univ. Chicago Press, 2000), 1098.
[256] Ibid., 832.

idiom."[257]

Hebrews 4:12 states, "For the Word of God is living and active, sharper than any two-edged sword, piercing to the division of soul and of spirit, of joints and of marrow, and discerning the thoughts and intentions of the heart" While virtually all trichotomists point to this text as evidence for their view, the term translated "division" (Grk. *merismos*) and its New Testament cognates always refer to the dividing up or distribution of the same thing.[258] For instance, Hebrews 2:14 speaks of "gifts of the Holy Spirit distributed (*merismos*) according to his will." Matthew 27:35 states, "And when they had crucified him, they divided (*dimerizo*) his garments among them by casting lots." Here, as in every occurrence of this verb, it is a single object that is being divided or better, distributed (cf. Luke 11:17-18; John 19:24).

ACADEMIC CHICANERY

In researching the Arnos, I attempted to examine their claims to considerable doctoral-level education credentials. Richard Arno claims to possess a "D.Psy." from Faith Theological Seminary, a Ph.D. from Andrew Jackson University, and a D.D. from Jacksonville Theological Seminary.[259] Mrs. Arno also claims to possess a Ph.D. from Andrew Jackson University.

My curiosity was piqued since "D.Psy" is not a

---

[257] Robert Letham, *Systematic Theology* (Wheaton, IL: Crossway, 2019), 340.

[258] John Murray, *Collected Writings of John Murray*, Vol. 2 (Carlisle, PA: Banner of Truth, 1982), 30.

[259] *National Christian Counselors Association: Licensing Program for Christian Counselors*, 52.

recognized abbreviation for the degree of Doctor of Psychology. To no avail, I attempted to locate the institution which issued this degree. I then attempted to verify the Arnos' Ph.D.s from Andrew Jackson University (AJU). This institution underwent a name change and is now New Charter University (NCU). NCU/AJU is a nationally accredited business college, offering only degrees in business and communications via distance education. Noticing that the school does not currently offer doctoral degrees, I inquired of NCU and asked the registrar if the school ever had a doctoral program. I was told that neither NCU nor AJU has ever had a doctoral degree program. Given that "Doctor of Divinity" is universally considered to be an honorary degree within the U.S., I've concluded that there is little reason to countenance the Arnos claims to doctoral-level education.

After developing creation therapy, the Arnos established the NCCA. This group provides training, credentials, and even degrees for those who desire to practice creation therapy. One can earn a "Bachelor of Arts in Christian Counseling" from NCCA by completing a mere fourteen courses![260] In the U.S., baccalaureate degrees require the equivalent of four years of full-time study. I contacted a school that is authorized to administer NCCA programs to inquire how long it would take for someone to earn a Bachelor of Arts from NCCA. I was told that one could earn this degree in as little as one year in full-time study. Needless to say, NCCA academic

---

[260] *National Christian Counselors Association: Licensing Program for Christian Counselors*, 22-5.

requirements are exceptionally substandard and meet the definition of a "diploma mill."[261]

CONCLUSION

Like LaHaye, the Arnos have done the church a fantastic disservice in purveying a completely unbiblical approach to helping hurting people. While the Arnos have sought to uphold the value of their modality by touting Creation Therapy's effectiveness, their counseling method is antithetical to Scripture. Creation Therapy was not founded upon a thoroughgoing exegesis of the Bible, but the pagan presuppositions of Galen and those who would build upon his lame theory. While the Arnos claim that Creation Therapy is "A Biblically Based Model for Christian Counseling," its tenets (e.g., the category of "temperament") are entirely foreign to the biblical text.

Functionally, the Arnos' system is detrimental to those that receive its counsel since it does not accord with the Bible's teaching. As shown above, NCCA counselors do not counsel people, but temperaments. The Arnos' system commodifies people and their problems, recasting them in a two-dimensional temperament framework.

---

[261] According to 20 US 1011, a "diploma mill" "offers, for a fee, degrees…[that require an] individual to complete little or no education or coursework." Cf. Higher Education Opportunity Act, §109.

About the Authors

Michael R. Burgos (Ph.D., Forge Theological Seminary) serves as pastor at Northwest Hills Community Church in Torrington, Connecticut where he resides with his wife Marion and their eight children. Michael is a certified counselor with the Association of Certified Biblical Counselors and has authored many books including *Our God is Triune: Essays in Biblical Theology* and *Against Oneness Pentecostalism:An Exegetical-Theological Critique* (3rd Ed.).

Chris Chumita is a certified counselor with the Association of Certified Biblical Counselors and is currently working toward an MA in Theological Studies at Covenant Baptist Theological Seminary. He is a member of Olmsted Falls Bible Church. Chris and his wife, Rachel, reside in Elyria, Ohio.